MAXIMS AND REFLECTIONS

MAXIMS
AND
REFLECTIONS

by

FRANCOIS DUC DE LA ROCHEFOUCAULD,
PRINCE DE MARSILLAC

Translated from the Editions of 1678 and 1827
by
J. W. Willis Bund, M.A. LL.B and J. Hain Friswell

with a Foreword by Mart
and Introduction by JL De L'Enclos

Translation first published 1871

This edition © 2022
Rogue Scholar Press
All Rights Reserved

Foreword © Mart
Introduction © JL De L'Enclos

ISBN: 978-1-954357-20-4

CONTENTS

Foreword

The works of François duc de La Rochefoucauld have attracted the attention of critics for more than three centuries; it has inspired the writing of more volumes and diverging interpretations than it contains maxims. His literary production consists of three parts: his letters, the Memoirs, and The Maxims, the latter being responsible for establishing him among the leading men of letters of his lifetime. Anyone studying La Rochefoucauld is tempted to suspect previous critiques of having chosen the wrong angle or interpretation; it is so because upon approaching the Maximes one thing is clear: arriving at a clear and straightforward understanding of the oeuvre is no easy task. The absence of architectural construction is evident—much like Pascal's *Pensées*, there's no logical order or criteria in the grouping of the aphorisms, although occasionally we may find a continuous series of maxims bearing on the same subject. The reader has therefore been warned that one will not find a carefully built, systematic work, nor an espousal for a certain system of ethics.

Instead this moraliste and darling of the salon provides us with a non-metaphysical and non-religious portrait of man within the social and natural world. Behind the author that he did not desire to be, that his rank even forbade him to be, we always discover in La Rochefoucauld a man, the man who had all the ambitions and at the same time sincerities and generosities, and who met only egoisms indifferent to all generosities and all sincerities; the man who, aged and forgotten, found consolation only in reflection, the man who had been able to realize himself, and who found success not in what had seemed to him the reasons to live, the battle, the victory, the power, but only in what for his equals had little value: the meditative intelligence and the esprit.

Although his aphorisms have an everlasting relevance and applicability, the genesis of La Rochefoucauld's works can be found in the time he lived in, the influence of the salon and his experiences as a disappointed Frondeur. As so often happens when calm returns after a period of great turbulence like that of a noble revolt opposing monarchical authority, the men who survive become, in the sudden silence, acutely conscious of themselves, of one another, and of the past experiences. That chaos and the malice of the Fronde, that expense of spirit, that period plagued with treachery and intrigues were responsible for his personal observations which would eventually become refined into aphorisms, although their abstract and precise style may conceal their concrete origins.

The Maximes are above all a psychological and moral work par excellence, man's nature is penetrated again and again by La Rochefoucauld's piercing gaze. If we investigate the actual content of the Maximes we will find that its main theme is not so different from that of Molière's *Tartuffe*: what looks like virtue is not; yet La Rochefoucauld takes his gloomy and pessimistic psychological and moral investigation even further. What passes for piety, clemency or constancy is nothing but a mere mask behind which lies temperament, passion, vanity and fear, magnanimity conceals ambition, politeness the desire to be well thought of. The demystifying thrust is deep and wounding, the heroic vision of man found in his contemporaries, Racine and Corneille, is directly attacked. This gentlemanly pessimistic vision of the human condition does acknowledge that ideal virtue, true love, true friendship might exist, but the overwhelming force of the collection is that the world is a place where *amour-propre* dominates, where commerce and self interest are the chief motivations and kindness, generosity, humility and all the other so-called virtues are in actuality means to further one's own interest; egoism, in short, is at the center of all human activity.

Friedrich Nietzsche can be credited with the twentieth-century renewed interest in the works of this seventeenth-century French aristocrat Duc François de la Rochefoucauld, for while in Nietzsche's time the Maximes were considered a mere product of the salon, and therefore superficial and trivial, Nietzsche saw great value in them, eventually shaping his psychological and moral observations (doesn't La Rochefoucauld's egoism become the stepping stone to Nietzsche's will to power?), as well as by his use of a particular literary genre: the aphorism. The style of the aphorism, maxim or apothegm, that style that Nietzsche admired in La Rochefoucauld and that has now become inextricably associated with his thought, can be traced back to the classical times, its main practitioners being Theognis of Megara, Hippocrates and Seneca.

The effect on Nietzsche is particularly relevant and noticeable in one of his main works: *Human All Too Human*, written between 1876 and 1878, and a work which would mark a crucial turning point in his thought, turning away from the Romanticism of Schopenhauer and Wagner. After the break with Richard Wagner, a new friend and philosophical stimulant came to the scene: Paul Rée, psychologist and the author of *Psychologische Beobachtungen*. The German Jew and Nietzsche entered into a friendship, which antagonized the Wagnerites and revealed Nietzsche's new positivistic orientations. It was at Rée's suggestion that Nietzsche began to read La Rochefoucauld, whom Rée admired enormously. While travelling to Sorrento, Nietzsche spent his spare time reading La Rochefoucauld's *Sentences et Maximes* on the train. In the first sections of his new work, Nietzsche immediately credits La Rochefoucauld with being his inspiration. Like the Frenchman, he too will now try his hand at "Sentenzen-Schleiferei", and indeed *Human All Too Human*, the most Gallic of all his writing, is the first of Nietzsche's works written in the aphoristic style. The philosopher-artist thus found a medium which could uphold the importance of both the aesthetic formulation and content of the written word, and for this end he subjected himself to countless workings and reworkings to achieve that characteristic staccato flair, featuring a precise brevity and stinging pithiness, which leaves the preliminary underpinnings of each thought unstated. In addition to this commonality, the literary style, one can distinguish their differences: La Rochefoucauld preferred the paradoxical aphorism, whereas Nietzsche's writing displays a more discursive aphoristic style, with the intention to clarify and lay out a matter in a definitive and aesthetic way; the German philosopher-artist deploys a powerful historical and genealogical approach to subjects whereas the Frenchman derives his knowledge from the concrete.

La Rochefoucauld's psychological and moral insights still ring true today, for a great thinker never grows old; he takes on different faces in the march of humanity, and when he was presumed to be old and outdated, he appears shining with a new youth. It is the privilege of a superior genius to force his readers to turn inward, either to approve or to refute him.

Mart

LA ROCHEFOUCAULD

The Life and Thoughts of La Rochefoucauld

JL De L'Enclos

On the night of July 1, 1652, the army of Louis de Bourbon, Prince de Condé passed around the northern outskirts of Paris, from the Porte Saint-Honoré in the west to the Porte Saint-Antoine in the east. Condé was the leading military commander of the rebellion known as the Fronde, which saw much of the French nobility rise up against the regency of Louis XIV under the queen mother Anne of Austria and the administration of Cardinal Mazarin—and he was in need of a more secure position. He had just met up with his army in the north, which was beset by difficulties, by sneaking through royalist lines along with the Duc de La Rochefoucauld and a handful of other followers. Now he was being pursued by two armies loyal to the King, each larger than his own: one belonging to the Vicomte de Turenne, and the other to the Maréchal de la Ferté.

Condé had resolved to move his army to Charenton in the east. His preference would have been to go south to Saint-Germain, but Gaston, the Duc d'Orleans and uncle of Louis XIV, was afraid a battle would take place outside the Palais de Luxembourg where he lived, and that his house would be struck by artillery fire. Lacking his consent to camp there, and reluctant to request passage through the city of Paris, which like the Duc d'Orleans was then wavering between the party of the Fronde and the party of the King, Condé made his move around the city walls. In so passing to the north, he and his army went directly by the royal Court, then sitting at Saint Denis, having previously decamped Paris under duress. The Court immediately became aware of his movement, and Turenne gave chase. We are told that the King himself went to watch the battle, which the Court expected to be the final defeat of Condé, and with that the end of the civil war.

Around seven o'clock in the morning, Condé reached the Faubourg Saint-Antoine, now part of the city of Paris, but at that time a suburb outside the city gates. It was then and there that Turenne caught up with Condé. Turenne initially sent a small detachment into Condé's rearguard, "to amuse him." As a result, the troops of Condé were thrown into disorder, and he had to abandon his baggage to have time to get his men in some semblance of order for battle. With his forces fragmented, Condé had immediately around himself no more than thirty or forty allied noblemen and members of his own household, whom he quickly formed into a squadron and moved to a defensive position behind some entrenchments the local villagers of the Faubourg had made several days earlier, expecting to be pillaged.

Turenne sent an entire well-ordered battalion against the small squadron, and it seemed to be the end for Condé in the eyes of those watching. But at thirty feet from their position, Condé charged out from his defensive entrenchments, sword in hand, whereupon he and his small band entirely defeated Turenne's battalion, taking their officers prisoner and capturing their banners before returning behind the entrenchments.

Nevertheless, Turenne's attacks continued, not only on Condé's immediate position but on his forces' other scattered positions as well. Yet the King's forces met intense resistance throughout the battle. Condé came out a second time from his entrenchments and once again repulsed Turenne's men. La Rochefoucauld tells us, "he was everywhere. And in the middle of the fire and the battle, he gave orders with that clarity of mind that is so rare and so necessary in these encounters."

After the second attack was repulsed, the rebel Duc de Beaufort joined up with Condé along with his brother-in-law, and rival Frondeur, the Duc de Nemours. Condé wanted to send his infantry against the musketry that had taken up positions in the houses along the road to Charenton. But Beaufort, disappointed that he had not fought alongside Condé at Turenne's two prior attacks while Nemours had, argued that they should instead attack the barricades blocking the road ahead. They proceeded with Beaufort's plan, but the attack failed and their infantry hid in hedges, no longer wishing to fight.

At this time La Rochefoucauld joined up with Beaufort and Nemours, and Beaufort proposed to the three of them that they and their followers attack a squadron of Flemish troops loyal to the King who were then passing down the road. It was a foolhardy attack, and they exposed themselves and their few companions who followed them to withering fire from the musketry in the houses lining the road.

But the guards at the barricade were put in shock by the boldness of the attack, and continuing to drive forward despite the musket fire from the houses, the noblemen pushed the guards back and took the barricade. Alone. Their followers had not joined them. Holding the barricade was nobody but the Duc de Beaufort, the Duc de Nemours, and the Duc de La Rochefoucauld, along with his eldest son François VII, Prince de Marcillac, who had just passed his eighteenth birthday a few weeks prior, and yet had already been in battle several times alongside his father over the past year.

Seeing that only four men held the barricade, the king's forces immediately counterattacked. Condé put himself in the road with his followers and tried to come to their aid, but the four noblemen were entirely outmatched. Nemours was shot 13 times. Most balls lodged in his armor, but several struck his body. La Rochefoucauld received a musket shot to the face. The ball passed behind one eye, into his nasal cavity, behind the other eye, and exited clean through the other side of his face. La Rochefoucauld tells us that he instantly lost sight. Beaufort and the young Marcillac helped the two wounded dukes to friendly lines, while Condé and his small squadron defended their retreat. The barricade was once again lost to the King's forces.

Both sides were by now exhausted by battle, and attention turned to the wounded, of which there were many on both sides. But word came that the King's other army, led by de la Ferté, was en route with fresh troops. Once again, it appeared to be the end for Condé and the Fronde.

But the opinion of the people of Paris suddenly shifted. They had up until that point viewed the battle cynically. Many mistrusted Condé, based on rumors of his previously attempting to make a separate peace with the King. Some even went so far as to think that the entire conflict was being staged by the King's chief minister, Cardinal Mazarin. But seeing so many dead and wounded noblemen being carried from the battlefield, such illusions were lost; and with their sympathy aroused, the Parisian people began to take the side of Condé.

The Duc d'Orleans, who held great sway over the city of Paris and controlled its defenses, had also wavered considerably between the two camps. Throughout the battle, the Cardinal de Retz continually counseled Orleans to remain neutral. But his twenty-five-year-old daughter, Anne Marie Louise, called la Grande Mademoiselle, overcame his indecision and took matters into her own hands. She went to the city hall and ordered the bourgeois of the city armed, so that they could remove the King's guard blocking the city gates. Then she went to the Bastille, which overlooked the battlefield, and ordered the governor of the fort to turn his cannon on the king's troops— which he did.

With the gates now open, La Rochefoucauld, despite his grave wounds, was helped onto his horse and rode into Paris, where he called on the people to join the side of Condé. La Grande Mademoiselle reported in her own *Mémoires* that she met him at the old Rue de Tissanderie (today the Rue de Rivoli, near the Hôtel de Ville). He was being held up on his horse by his son the Prince de Marcillac and his right-hand man, Jean Hérauld Gourville. All three men had on white doublets, which were covered in the duke's blood. La Rochefoucauld was exhaling heavily, for fear that the blood running from his nose into his mouth would suffocate him. And it appeared, she said, that his eyes were falling out of his head. She did not think he would be able to survive.

Following the swing in popular support and the intervention of la Grande Mademoiselle, Condé entered the city to great acclamation, despite being grossly outmatched and having endured heavy casualties. It was a sort of triumphal retreat into Paris. The captured banners of Turenne and others were hung up on the Cathedral of Notre Dame. Condé was at the height of his power. The King and Court returned to their provisional seat at St. Denis.

But by October, after various duels, riots, melees, and other intrigues, the Fronde collapsed and the civil war was over. The King retook Paris with Turenne's assistance, and Condé went into in exile. La Rochefoucauld survived, and the King offered him amnesty. But he refused it, and chose instead to recuperate from his wounds with his family far away from Paris, near Luxembourg in lands governed by his brother-in-law.

Married at fifteen, a soldier from sixteen, a father at twenty, and exiled from court once previously at the age twenty-one for "imprudence of language," no written work had yet appeared in print under La Rochefoucauld's name, and nothing out of print besides some letters. Now, at thirty-nine years old, the cause he had fought for was lost; his injuries would require a lengthy convalescence; his affairs were in disarray after years of war; his family seat, the Chateau de Verteuil, had been leveled by the

King's forces; and he was out of favor with the Court once again.

Yet it is in this second exile, during his recuperation from the wounds of war and the rebuilding of a shattered noble house, that we encounter one of the most remarkable moralists that the European spirit has produced in any age.

"Hypocrisy is the homage vice pays to virtue."

"Nothing is given so profusely as advice."

"The head is ever the dupe of the heart."

"Neither the sun nor death can be looked at without blinking."

"Quarrels would not last long if the fault was only on one side."

"We are never so happy or so unhappy as we suppose."

When one encounters the maxims of La Rochefoucauld, they are typically of the sort translated above. The kinds of pithy turns of phrase that used to occasionally leaven the writings of essayists and the speech of political men, before the quality of our public discourse degraded to its present state. Yet the *Réflexions ou Sentences et Maximes Morales* are more than pithy turns of phrase. They contain a system. But not a system of philosophy (for which La Rochefoucauld holds a certain contempt).

"Philosophy triumphs easily over past evils and future evils; but present evils triumph over it." (22)

Rather, they contain a system of moral psychology that distills and crystalizes and isolates and refines human nature into its constituent elements, and reassembles them into a picture of man as he truly is, even if it is not what theologians or philosophers might hope.

"Vices enter into the composition of virtues as poison into that of medicines. Prudence collects and blends the two and renders them useful against the ills of life." (182)

Nietzsche, praising both the maxim as a literary form and the author of these, called them "accurately aimed arrows, which hit the mark again and again, the black mark of man's nature." The metaphor of the arrow is apt, but not ideal. Better to liken the *Maximes* to the epée:

"Gravity is a mysterious carriage of the body invented to conceal the want of mind." (257)

or to the musket:

"No one should be praised for his goodness if he has not strength enough to be wicked. All other goodness is but too often an idleness or powerlessness of will." (237)

The maxim is the perfect literary form for a man of the *noblesse de l'epée* who was willing to go to war against his own King in order to protect his privileges, to maintain his rule over his ancestral domains—and, indeed, for the love of adventure and intrigue. It is pure assertion. Unsupported by argument or data, it is its own evidence. It is the literary equivalent of the thrust of a blade or the blast of a gun. His maxims are frequently cutting, often ironic, and occasionally quite funny:

"The greater number of good women are like concealed treasures, safe as no one has searched for them." (368)

He fights with the pen just as he did at the battle of Faubourg Saint-Antoine, like a true French nobleman—among the few, exposed to enemy fire, but bravely staking his claim with a bold and contentious pronouncement.

"What men term friendship is merely a partnership with a collection of reciprocal interests, and an exchange of favours—in fact it is but a trade in which self-love always expects to gain something." (83)

No longer at war, and in repose, he wages a battle of the mind's wit. It must be understood that the maxims are the product of aristocratic conversation —the intrigue and hypocrisy of court, of course; but also: the salon, letters, and above all liaisons and affairs and private friendships, especially with young women. The quintessential image of La Rochefoucauld is the convalescing nobleman reclining at one of his estates while conversing intently with two pretty girls in finery. In the years after the Fronde, he became closely linked with Mme de Sévigné, author of celebrated letters to her daughter, and Mme de Lafayette, author of perhaps the first truly modern novel, *La Princesse de Clèves*.

Without a doubt, La Rochefoucauld has his enemies. They existed in his day and persist throughout literary history, and they follow a certain fixed line of attack. That line is very well exemplified in a biographical work by the minor 19th century French philosopher Victor Cousin. He takes up the early life of the duchesse de Longueville, who was the sister of Condé, mistress of La Rochefoucauld, and the central figure in the political intrigues that initiated and sustained the Fronde. Cousin paints a picture of La Rochefoucauld as entirely self-interested and totally lacking in virtue—particularly lacking in the virtues of courtly love.

To his way of thinking, La Rochefoucauld should have put Mme de Longueville on a pedestal and sacrificed himself for her sake, rather than manipulating her into leading the Fronde and using his relations with her for personal and political advantages—and then casting her aside at the merest hint of betrayal.

La Rochefoucauld suspected Mme de Longueville of having secretly entered into an affair with the Duc de Nemours, and said as much in his *Mémoires*. Although they were published anonymously and he disavowed authorship, the accusation made a scandal; and that, along with the collapse of the Fronde, drove Mme de Longueville to spend the rest of her life at the abbey of Port-Royal in religious seclusion. La Rochefoucauld, meanwhile, healed from his wounds and regained his sight, reentered the King's favor and gained high offices for himself and his sons, and joined a literary society where he circulated works that gained great and lasting renown.

"In love the quickest is always the best cure." (417)

Cousin's line of attack is heavily influenced by the unflattering depiction of La Rochefoucauld recorded by his fellow Frondeur and bitterest rival: Paul de Gondi, Cardinal de Retz. Retz is the author of celebrated *Mémoires*, which contain a sardonically belittling portrait of La Rochefoucauld. Retz describes him as possessed of good qualities but habitually vacillating and never able to carry matters to a profitable outcome; a soldier but not a warrior; and author of the *Maximes* which show insufficient faith in virtue:

"he would have done better to know himself and reduce himself to passing, as he could have done, for the most polished courtier of his century."

La Rochefoucauld for his part responded with a written portrait of Retz which was substantially more direct and caustic: "little piety, some appearance of religion"; "seems ambitious without being it"; "insensitive to hatred and friendship, whatever care he took to look busy with the one or the other." His contempt is not surprising. At one point in the Fronde, La Rochefoucauld tried to assassinate Retz, then insulted him in front of the Parliament of Paris, and would have dueled with him over it, had it not been for the intervention of the Duc d'Orleans.

The critics do have some merit to their charges. La Rochefoucauld was, without a doubt, a political and economic failure in the first part of his life. Although he inherited a ducal title and was a hereditary pair de France, his early love of intrigue and adventure left his house in tatters.

"Youth is a continual intoxication; it is the fever of reason." (271)

But it was through his engagement in affairs that La Rochefoucauld developed a penetrating sense of the psychological motives that drive human action.

"Men and things have each their proper perspective; to judge rightly of some it is necessary to see them near, of others we can never judge rightly but at a distance." (104)

And in the system of La Rochefoucauld, affairs are nothing more than the actions of particular men, who are driven by their own interests, including their interest in honor and glory; their pride or self-love; their individual humors or dispositions; and above all, fortune.

"What we term virtue is often but a mass of various actions and divers interests, which fortune, or our own industry, manage to arrange; and it is not always from valour or from chastity that men are brave, and women chaste." (1)

La Rochefoucauld is not seeking with the *Maximes* to raise man to the attainment of a higher condition. But nor is he an amoralist or moral anarchist,

instructing followers to abandon virtue. He is the
engaged spectator, the mature aristocrat who, having
passed from an active life to a largely contemplative
one, is able to see in others and in himself the bitter
truth of man's high moral aspirations when they
confront reality.

*"As rivers are lost in the sea so are virtues in
self."* (171)

And neither he is a Machiavellian, inventing new
modes and orders, nor is he a Nietzschean affecting a
transvaluation of values. The system of La
Rochefoucauld is not one of social or political
improvement or even criticism. It is directed above
all at affecting the most penetrating possible insight
into the mind and motives of men...

*"The greatest mistake of penetration is not to have
fallen short, but to have gone too far."* (377)

...while leaving the rest to fortune.

*"Fortune makes visible our virtues or our vices, as light
does objects."* (380)

Nature and fortune are the two great givens for
La Rochefoucauld, with nature being the material
and fortune being the field of action—each of which
serve to distinguish men.

"Nature makes merit but fortune sets it to work." (153)

La Rochefoucauld speaks of fortune the way many of his contemporaries would speak of Providence, which he only referred to once, in an early edition of the *Maximes.*

"Whatever variety and change appears in the world, we may remark a secret chain, and a regulated order of all time by Providence, which makes everything follow in due rank and fall into its destined course." (XXXIX, 613, 225 in 1665 ed.)

He removed that maxim in subsequent editions, and in view of the overall system, we can see why it was suppressed. La Rochefoucauld assiduously avoids allowing any sort of hidden hand or guiding mechanism, other than fortune, to enter into his portrayal of human motivations. And yet even fortune is not entirely determinative.

"There is a kind of greatness which does not depend upon fortune: it is a certain manner what distinguishes us, and which seems to destine us for great things; it is the value we insensibly set upon ourselves; it is by this quality that we gain the deference of other men, and it is this which commonly raises us more above them, than birth, rank, or even merit itself." (399)

It is a view that sees man as fundamentally active according to his nature—not as a reactive object of group dynamics or as a passive observer of a deterministic historical process. And even though fortune as well as nature must favor those who wish to win eternal fame...

"Whatever great advantages nature may give, it is not she alone, but fortune also that makes the hero." (53)

...great men know how to make fortune favor them.

"To be a great man one should know how to profit by every phase of fortune." (343)

These maxims, although they were published in multiple editions and were well-known in his lifetime, reflect the preoccupations of a nobleman. They are not the sort of thoughts that are appropriate for the many.

"Ordinary men commonly condemn what is beyond them." (375)

Nietzsche recognized as much in his encounter with La Rochefoucauld, wondering whether "perhaps the belief in goodness, in virtuous men and actions, in an abundance of impersonal goodwill in the world has made men better." He goes on to "table the question of whether psychological observation brings more advantage or harm upon men."

La Rochefoucauld, however, does not entirely avoid that question. In the final maxim, he addresses the fear of death and the falsehood and self-deception of those who appear to disdain it— regardless of their status.

"... whatever difference there may be between the peer and the peasant, we have constantly seen both the one and the other meet death with the same composure. Still there

*is always this difference, that the contempt the peer shows
for death is but the love of fame which hides death from his
sight; in the peasant it is but the result of his limited vision
that hides from him the extent of the evil, end leaves him
free to reflect on other things."* (504)

It is a striking yet altogether fitting coda to the
Maximes, and one which stands as a rebuke to some
of the basic presumptions that pervade the present
epoch. At a minimum, we ought to doubt that La
Rochefoucauld would recognize the merit of pressing
the common man into a scheme of universal
education, thereby stealing from him that simplicity
of spirit which is his succor from life's greatest evil,
and arousing in him instead the false hope of social
progress and technological improvement.

Worse than misguided schemes to raise the social
and intellectual condition of the common man,
which continue to fail despite centuries of effort, is
the nagging sense that an overall decline in human
substance and an oppressive empire of petty
regulation of daily life are reaching a point where we
may never again see great men. But La
Rochefoucauld reminds us that the reluctant warrior
and the bureaucrat were with him in his day also.

*"We do not wish to lose life; we do wish to gain glory,
and this makes brave men show more tact and address in
avoiding death, than rogues show in preserving their
fortunes."* (221)

And so too was the impulse of the unremarkable
masses to hinder and constrain the great.

"Moderation is made a virtue to limit the ambition of the great; to console ordinary people for their small fortune and equally small ability." (308)

Yet the desire for glory never dies in the hearts of certain men—the best men. As inhospitable as the times are to the pursuit of glory, so much greater will be the faculties and so much bolder will be the enterprises of those immoderate men who aspire to ever-flowing renown among mortals. And that will make their names all the greater.

"The fame of great men ought always to be estimated by the means used to acquire it." (157)

REFLECTIONS;
OR, SENTENCES
AND MORAL MAXIMS

Our virtues are most frequently but vices disguised.

1.—What we term virtue is often but a mass of various actions and divers interests, which fortune, or our own industry, manage to arrange; and it is not always from valour or from chastity that men are brave, and women chaste.

2.—Self-love is the greatest of flatterers.

3.—Whatever discoveries have been made in the region of self-love, there remain many unexplored territories there.

4.—Self love is more cunning than the most cunning man in the world.

5.—The duration of our passions is no more dependant upon us than the duration of our life.

6.—Passion often renders the most clever man a fool, and even sometimes renders the most foolish man clever.

7.—Great and striking actions which dazzle the eyes are represented by politicians as the effect of great designs, instead of which they are commonly caused by the temper and the passions. Thus the war between Augustus and Anthony, which is set down to the ambition they entertained of making themselves masters of the world, was probably but an effect of jealousy.

8.—The passions are the only advocates which always persuade. They are a natural art, the rules of which are infallible; and the simplest man with passion will be more persuasive than the most eloquent without.

9.—The passions possess a certain injustice and self interest which makes it dangerous to follow them, and in reality we should distrust them even when they appear most trustworthy.

10.—In the human heart there is a perpetual generation of passions; so that the ruin of one is almost always the foundation of another.

11.—Passions often produce their contraries: avarice sometimes leads to prodigality, and prodigality to avarice; we are often obstinate through weakness and daring though timidity.

12.—Whatever care we take to conceal our passions under the appearances of piety and honour, they are always to be seen through these veils.

13.—Our self love endures more impatiently the condemnation of our tastes than of our opinions.

14.—Men are not only prone to forget benefits and injuries; they even hate those who have obliged them, and cease to hate those who have injured them. The necessity of revenging an injury or of recompensing a benefit seems a slavery to which they are unwilling to submit.

15.—The clemency of Princes is often but policy to win the affections of the people.

16.—This clemency of which they make a merit, arises oftentimes from vanity, sometimes from idleness, oftentimes from fear, and almost always from all three combined.

17.—The moderation of those who are happy arises from the calm which good fortune bestows upon their temper.

18.—Moderation is caused by the fear of exciting the envy and contempt which those merit who are intoxicated with their good fortune; it is a vain display of our strength of mind, and in short the moderation of men at their greatest height is only a desire to appear greater than their fortune.

19.—We have all sufficient strength to support the misfortunes of others.

20.—The constancy of the wise is only the talent of concealing the agitation of their hearts.

21.—Those who are condemned to death affect sometimes a constancy and contempt for death which is only the fear of facing it; so that one may say that this constancy and contempt are to their mind what the bandage is to their eyes.

22.—Philosophy triumphs easily over past evils and future evils; but present evils triumph over it.

23.—Few people know death, we only endure it, usually from determination, and even from stupidity and custom; and most men only die because they know not how to prevent dying.

24.—When great men permit themselves to be cast down by the continuance of misfortune, they show us that they were only sustained by ambition, and not by their mind; so that PLUS a great vanity, heroes are made like other men.

25.—We need greater virtues to sustain good than evil fortune.

26.—Neither the sun nor death can be looked at without blinking.

27.—People are often vain of their passions, even of the worst, but envy is a passion so timid and shame-faced that no one ever dare avow her.

28.—Jealousy is in a manner just and reasonable, as it tends to preserve a good which belongs, or which we believe belongs to us, on the other hand envy is a fury which cannot endure the happiness of others.

29.—The evil that we do does not attract to us so much persecution and hatred as our good qualities.

30.—We have more strength than will; and it is often merely for an excuse we say things are impossible.

31.—If we had no faults we should not take so much pleasure in noting those of others.

32.—Jealousy lives upon doubt; and comes to an end or becomes a fury as soon as it passes from doubt to certainty.

33.—Pride indemnifies itself and loses nothing even when it casts away vanity.

34.—If we had no pride we should not complain of that of others.

35.—Pride is much the same in all men, the only difference is the method and manner of showing it.

36.—It would seem that nature, which has so wisely ordered the organs of our body for our happiness, has also given us pride to spare us the mortification of knowing our imperfections.

37.—Pride has a larger part than goodness in our remonstrances with those who commit faults, and we reprove them not so much to correct as to persuade them that we ourselves are free from faults.

38.—We promise according to our hopes; we perform according to our fears.

39.—Interest speaks all sorts of tongues and plays all sorts of characters; even that of disinterestedness.

40.—Interest blinds some and makes some see.

41.—Those who apply themselves too closely to little things often become incapable of great things.

42.—We have not enough strength to follow all our reason.

43.—A man often believes himself leader when he is led; as his mind endeavours to reach one goal, his heart insensibly drags him towards another.

44.—Strength and weakness of mind are misnamed; they are really only the good or happy arrangement of our bodily organs.

45.—The caprice of our temper is even more whimsical than that of Fortune.

46.—The attachment or indifference which philosophers have shown to life is only the style of their self love, about which we can no more dispute than of that of the palate or of the choice of colours.

47.—Our temper sets a price upon every gift that we receive from fortune.

48.—Happiness is in the taste, and not in the things themselves; we are happy from possessing what we like, not from possessing what others like.

49.—We are never so happy or so unhappy as we suppose.

50.—Those who think they have merit persuade themselves that they are honoured by being unhappy, in order to persuade others and themselves that they are worthy to be the butt of fortune.

51.—Nothing should so much diminish the satisfaction which we feel with ourselves as seeing that we disapprove at one time of that which we approve of at another.

52.—Whatever difference there appears in our fortunes, there is nevertheless a certain compensation of good and evil which renders them equal.

53.—Whatever great advantages nature may give, it is not she alone, but fortune also that makes the hero.

54.—The contempt of riches in philosophers was only a hidden desire to avenge their merit upon the injustice of fortune, by despising the very goods of which fortune had deprived them; it was a secret to guard themselves against the degradation of poverty, it was a back way by which to arrive at that distinction which they could not gain by riches.

55.—The hate of favourites is only a love of favour. The envy of NOT possessing it, consoles and softens its regrets by the contempt it evinces for those who possess it, and we refuse them our homage, not being able to detract from them what attracts that of the rest of the world.

56.—To establish ourselves in the world we do everything to appear as if we were established.

57.—Although men flatter themselves with their great actions, they are not so often the result of a great design as of chance.

58.—It would seem that our actions have lucky or unlucky stars to which they owe a great part of the blame or praise which is given them.

59.—There are no accidents so unfortunate from which skilful men will not draw some advantage, nor so fortunate that foolish men will not turn them to their hurt.

60.—Fortune turns all things to the advantage of those on whom she smiles.

61.—The happiness or unhappiness of men depends no less upon their dispositions than their fortunes.

62.—Sincerity is an openness of heart; we find it in very few people; what we usually see is only an artful dissimulation to win the confidence of others.

63.—The aversion to lying is often a hidden ambition to render our words credible and weighty, and to attach a religious aspect to our conversation.

64.—Truth does not do as much good in the world, as its counterfeits do evil.

65.—There is no praise we have not lavished upon Prudence; and yet she cannot assure to us the most trifling event.

66.—A clever man ought to so regulate his interests that each will fall in due order. Our greediness so often troubles us, making us run after so many things at the same time, that while we too eagerly look after the least we miss the greatest.

67.—What grace is to the body good sense is to the mind.

68.—It is difficult to define love; all we can say is, that in the soul it is a desire to rule, in the mind it is a sympathy, and in the body it is a hidden and delicate wish to possess what we love—*Plus* many mysteries.

69.—If there is a pure love, exempt from the mixture of our other passions, it is that which is concealed at the bottom of the heart and of which even ourselves are ignorant.

70.—There is no disguise which can long hide love where it exists, nor feign it where it does not.

71.—There are few people who would not be ashamed of being beloved when they love no longer.

72.—If we judge of love by the majority of its results it rather resembles hatred than friendship.

73.—We may find women who have never indulged in an intrigue, but it is rare to find those who have intrigued but once.

74.—There is only one sort of love, but there are a thousand different copies.

75.—Neither love nor fire can subsist without perpetual motion; both cease to live so soon as they cease to hope, or to fear.

76.—There is real love just as there are real ghosts; every person speaks of it, few persons have seen it.

77.—Love lends its name to an infinite number of engagements (*Commerces*) which are attributed to it, but with which it has no more concern than the Doge has with all that is done in Venice.

78.—The love of justice is simply in the majority of men the fear of suffering injustice.

79.—Silence is the best resolve for him who distrusts himself.

80.—What renders us so changeable in our friendship is, that it is difficult to know the qualities of the soul, but easy to know those of the mind.

81.—We can love nothing but what agrees with us, and we can only follow our taste or our pleasure when we prefer our friends to ourselves;

nevertheless it is only by that preference that friendship can be true and perfect.

82.—Reconciliation with our enemies is but a desire to better our condition, a weariness of war, the fear of some unlucky accident.

83.—What men term friendship is merely a partnership with a collection of reciprocal interests, and an exchange of favours—in fact it is but a trade in which self love always expects to gain something.

84.—It is more disgraceful to distrust than to be deceived by our friends.

85.—We often persuade ourselves to love people who are more powerful than we are, yet interest alone produces our friendship; we do not give our hearts away for the good we wish to do, but for that we expect to receive.

86.—Our distrust of another justifies his deceit.

87.—Men would not live long in society were they not the dupes of each other.

88.—Self love increases or diminishes for us the good qualities of our friends, in proportion to the satisfaction we feel with them, and we judge of their merit by the manner in which they act towards us.

89.—Everyone blames his memory, no one blames his judgment.

90.—In the intercourse of life, we please more by our faults than by our good qualities.

91.—The largest ambition has the least appearance of ambition when it meets with an absolute impossibility in compassing its object.

92.—To awaken a man who is deceived as to his own merit is to do him as bad a turn as that done to the Athenian madman who was happy in believing that all the ships touching at the port belonged to him.

93.—Old men delight in giving good advice as a consolation for the fact that they can no longer set bad examples.

94.—Great names degrade instead of elevating those who know not how to sustain them.

95.—The test of extraordinary merit is to see those who envy it the most yet obliged to praise it.

96.—A man is perhaps ungrateful, but often less chargeable with ingratitude than his benefactor is.

97.—We are deceived if we think that mind and judgment are two different matters: judgment is but the extent of the light of the mind. This light penetrates to the bottom of matters; it remarks all that can be remarked, and perceives what appears imperceptible. Therefore we must agree that it is the extent of the light in the mind that produces all the effects which we attribute to judgment.

98.—Everyone praises his heart, none dare praise their understanding.

99.—Politeness of mind consists in thinking chaste and refined thoughts.

100.—Gallantry of mind is saying the most empty things in an agreeable manner.

101.—Ideas often flash across our minds more complete than we could make them after much labour.

102.—The head is ever the dupe of the heart.

103.—Those who know their minds do not necessarily know their hearts.

104.—Men and things have each their proper perspective; to judge rightly of some it is necessary to see them near, of others we can never judge rightly but at a distance.

105.—A man for whom accident discovers sense, is not a rational being. A man only is so who understands, who distinguishes, who tests it.

106.—To understand matters rightly we should understand their details, and as that knowledge is almost infinite, our knowledge is always superficial and imperfect.

107.—One kind of flirtation is to boast we never flirt.

108.—The head cannot long play the part of the heart.

109.—Youth changes its tastes by the warmth of its blood, age retains its tastes by habit.

110.—Nothing is given so profusely as advice.

111.—The more we love a woman the more prone we are to hate her.

112.—The blemishes of the mind, like those of the face, increase by age.

113.—There may be good but there are no pleasant marriages.

114.—We are inconsolable at being deceived by our enemies and betrayed by our friends, yet still we are often content to be thus served by ourselves.

115.—It is as easy unwittingly to deceive oneself as to deceive others.

116.—Nothing is less sincere than the way of asking and giving advice. The person asking seems to pay deference to the opinion of his friend, while thinking in reality of making his friend approve his opinion and be responsible for his conduct. The person giving the advice returns the confidence placed in him by eager and disinterested zeal, in doing which he is usually guided only by his own interest or reputation.

117.—The most subtle of our acts is to simulate blindness for snares that we know are set for us. We are never so easily deceived as when trying to deceive.

118.—The intention of never deceiving often exposes us to deception.

119.—We become so accustomed to disguise ourselves to others that at last we are disguised to ourselves.

120.—We often act treacherously more from weakness than from a fixed motive.

121.—We frequently do good to enable us with impunity to do evil.

122.—If we conquer our passions it is more from their weakness than from our strength.

123.—If we never flattered ourselves we should have but scant pleasure.

124.—The most deceitful persons spend their lives in blaming deceit, so as to use it on some great occasion to promote some great interest.

125.—The daily employment of cunning marks a little mind, it generally happens that those who resort to it in one respect to protect themselves lay themselves open to attack in another.

126.—Cunning and treachery are the offspring of incapacity.

127.—The true way to be deceived is to think oneself more knowing than others.

128.—Too great cleverness is but deceptive delicacy, true delicacy is the most substantial cleverness.

129.—It is sometimes necessary to play the fool to avoid being deceived by cunning men.

130.—Weakness is the only fault which cannot be cured.

131.—The smallest fault of women who give themselves up to love is to love.

132.—It is far easier to be wise for others than to be so for oneself.

133.—The only good examples are those, that make us see the absurdity of bad originals.

134.—We are never so ridiculous from the habits we have as from those that we affect to have.

135.—We sometimes differ more widely from ourselves than we do from others.

136.—There are some who never would have loved if they never had heard it spoken of.

137.—When not prompted by vanity we say little.

138.—A man would rather say evil of himself than say nothing.

139.—One of the reasons that we find so few persons rational and agreeable in conversation is there is hardly a person who does not think more of what he wants to say than of his answer to what is said. The most clever and polite are content with only seeming attentive while we perceive in their mind and eyes that at the very time they are wandering from what is said and desire to return to what they want to say. Instead of considering that the worst way to persuade or please others is to try thus strongly to please ourselves, and that to listen well and to answer well are some of the greatest charms we can have in conversation.

140.—If it was not for the company of fools, a witty man would often be greatly at a loss.

141.—We often boast that we are never bored, but yet we are so conceited that we do not perceive how often we bore others.

142.—As it is the mark of great minds to say many things in a few words, so it is that of little minds to use many words to say nothing.

143.—It is oftener by the estimation of our own feelings that we exaggerate the good qualities of others than by their merit, and when we praise them we wish to attract their praise.

144.—We do not like to praise, and we never praise without a motive. Praise is flattery, artful, hidden, delicate, which gratifies differently him who praises and him who is praised. The one takes it as the reward of merit, the other bestows it to show his impartiality and knowledge.

145.—We often select envenomed praise which, by a reaction upon those we praise, shows faults we could not have shown by other means.

146.—Usually we only praise to be praised.

147.—Few are sufficiently wise to prefer censure which is useful to praise which is treacherous.

148.—Some reproaches praise; some praises reproach.

149.—The refusal of praise is only the wish to be praised twice.

150.—The desire which urges us to deserve praise strengthens our good qualities, and praise given to wit, valour, and beauty, tends to increase them.

151.—It is easier to govern others than to prevent being governed.

152.—If we never flattered ourselves the flattery of others would not hurt us.

153.—Nature makes merit but fortune sets it to work.

154.—Fortune cures us of many faults that reason could not.

155.—There are some persons who only disgust with their abilities, there are persons who please even with their faults.

156.—There are persons whose only merit consists in saying and doing stupid things at the right time, and who ruin all if they change their manners.

157.—The fame of great men ought always to be estimated by the means used to acquire it.

158.—Flattery is base coin to which only our vanity gives currency.

159.—It is not enough to have great qualities, we should also have the management of them.

160.—However brilliant an action it should not be esteemed great unless the result of a great motive.

161.—A certain harmony should be kept between actions and ideas if we desire to estimate the effects that they produce.

162.—The art of using moderate abilities to advantage wins praise, and often acquires more reputation than real brilliancy.

163.—Numberless arts appear foolish whose secret motives are most wise and weighty.

164.—It is much easier to seem fitted for posts we do not fill than for those we do.

165.—Ability wins us the esteem of the true men, luck that of the people.

166.—The world oftener rewards the appearance of merit than merit itself.

167.—Avarice is more opposed to economy than to liberality.

168.—However deceitful hope may be, yet she carries us on pleasantly to the end of life.

169.—Idleness and fear keeps us in the path of duty, but our virtue often gets the praise.

170.—If one acts rightly and honestly, it is difficult to decide whether it is the effect of integrity or skill.

171.—As rivers are lost in the sea so are virtues in self.

172.—If we thoroughly consider the varied effects of indifference we find we miscarry more in our duties than in our interests.

173.—There are different kinds of curiosity: one springs from interest, which makes us desire to know everything that may be profitable to us; another from pride, which springs from a desire of knowing what others are ignorant of.

174.—It is far better to accustom our mind to bear the ills we have than to speculate on those which may befall us.

175.—Constancy in love is a perpetual inconstancy which causes our heart to attach itself to all the qualities of the person we love in succession, sometimes giving the preference to one, sometimes to another. This constancy is merely inconstancy fixed, and limited to the same person.

176.—There are two kinds of constancy in love, one arising from incessantly finding in the loved one fresh objects to love, the other from regarding it as a point of honour to be constant.

177.—Perseverance is not deserving of blame or praise, as it is merely the continuance of tastes and feelings which we can neither create or destroy.

178.—What makes us like new studies is not so much the weariness we have of the old or the wish for change as the desire to be admired by those who know more than ourselves, and the hope of advantage over those who know less.

179.—We sometimes complain of the levity of our friends to justify our own by anticipation.

180.—Our repentance is not so much sorrow for the ill we have done as fear of the ill that may happen to us.

181.—One sort of inconstancy springs from levity or weakness of mind, and makes us accept everyone's opinion, and another more excusable comes from a surfeit of matter.

182.—Vices enter into the composition of virtues as poison into that of medicines. Prudence collects and blends the two and renders them useful against the ills of life.

183.—For the credit of virtue we must admit that the greatest misfortunes of men are those into which they fall through their crimes.

184.—We admit our faults to repair by our sincerity the evil we have done in the opinion of others.

185.—There are both heroes of evil and heroes of good.

186.—We do not despise all who have vices, but we do despise all who have not virtues.

187.—The name of virtue is as useful to our interest as that of vice.

188.—The health of the mind is not less uncertain than that of the body, and when passions seem furthest removed we are no less in danger of infection than of falling ill when we are well.

189.—It seems that nature has at man's birth fixed the bounds of his virtues and vices.

190.—Great men should not have great faults.

191.—We may say vices wait on us in the course of our life as the landlords with whom we successively lodge, and if we travelled the road twice over I doubt if our experience would make us avoid them.

192.—When our vices leave us we flatter ourselves with the idea we have left them.

193.—There are relapses in the diseases of the mind as in those of the body; what we call a cure is often no more than an intermission or change of disease.

194.—The defects of the mind are like the wounds of the body. Whatever care we take to heal them the scars ever remain, and there is always danger of their reopening.

195.—The reason which often prevents us abandoning a single vice is having so many.

196.—We easily forget those faults which are known only to ourselves.

197.—There are men of whom we can never believe evil without having seen it. Yet there are very few in whom we should be surprised to see it.

198.—We exaggerate the glory of some men to detract from that of others, and we should praise Prince Condé and Marshal Turenne much less if we did not want to blame them both.

199.—The desire to appear clever often prevents our being so.

200.—Virtue would not go far did not vanity escort her.

201.—He who thinks he has the power to content the world greatly deceives himself, but he who thinks that the world cannot be content with him deceives himself yet more.

202.—Falsely honest men are those who disguise their faults both to themselves and others; truly honest men are those who know them perfectly and confess them.

203.—He is really wise who is nettled at nothing.

204.—The coldness of women is a balance and burden they add to their beauty.

205.—Virtue in woman is often the love of reputation and repose.

206.—He is a truly good man who desires always to bear the inspection of good men.

207.—Folly follows us at all stages of life. If one appears wise it is but because his folly is proportioned to his age and fortune.

208.—There are foolish people who know and who skilfully use their folly.

209.—Who lives without folly is not so wise as he thinks.

210.—In growing old we become more foolish—and more wise.

211.—There are people who are like farces, which are praised but for a time (however foolish and distasteful they may be).

212.—Most people judge men only by success or by fortune.

213.—Love of glory, fear of shame, greed of fortune, the desire to make life agreeable and comfortable, and the wish to depreciate others are often causes of that bravery so vaunted among men.

214.—Valour in common soldiers is a perilous method of earning their living.

215.—Perfect bravery and sheer cowardice are two extremes rarely found. The space between them is vast, and embraces all other sorts of courage. The difference between them is not less than between faces and tempers. Men will freely expose themselves at the beginning of an action, and relax and be easily discouraged if it should last. Some are content to satisfy worldly honour, and beyond that will do little else. Some are not always equally masters of their timidity. Others allow themselves to be overcome by panic; others charge because they dare not remain at their posts. Some may be found whose courage is strengthened by small perils, which prepare them to face greater dangers. Some will dare a sword cut and flinch from a bullet; others dread bullets little and fear to fight with swords. These varied kinds of courage agree in this, that night, by increasing fear and concealing gallant or cowardly actions, allows men to spare themselves. There is even a more general discretion to be observed, for we meet with no man who does all he would have done if he were assured of getting off scot-free; so that it is certain that the fear of death does somewhat subtract from valour.

216.—Perfect valour is to do without witnesses what one would do before all the world.

217.—Intrepidity is an extraordinary strength of soul which raises it above the troubles, disorders, and emotions which the sight of great perils can arouse in it: by this strength heroes maintain a calm aspect and preserve their reason and liberty in the most surprising and terrible accidents.

218.—Hypocrisy is the homage vice pays to virtue.

219.—Most men expose themselves in battle enough to save their honor, few wish to do so more than sufficiently, or than is necessary to make the design for which they expose themselves succeed.

220.—Vanity, shame, and above all disposition, often make men brave and women chaste.

221.—We do not wish to lose life; we do wish to gain glory, and this makes brave men show more tact and address in avoiding death, than rogues show in preserving their fortunes.

222.—Few persons on the first approach of age do not show wherein their body, or their mind, is beginning to fail.

223.—Gratitude is as the good faith of merchants: it holds commerce together; and we do not pay because it is just to pay debts, but because we shall thereby more easily find people who will lend.

224.—All those who pay the debts of gratitude cannot thereby flatter themselves that they are grateful.

225.—What makes false reckoning, as regards gratitude, is that the pride of the giver and the receiver cannot agree as to the value of the benefit.

226.—Too great a hurry to discharge of an obligation is a kind of ingratitude.

227.—Lucky people are bad hands at correcting their faults; they always believe that they are right when fortune backs up their vice or folly.

228.—Pride will not owe, self-love will not pay.

229.—The good we have received from a man should make us excuse the wrong he does us.

230.—Nothing is so infectious as example, and we never do great good or evil without producing the like. We imitate good actions by emulation, and bad ones by the evil of our nature, which shame imprisons until example liberates.

231.—It is great folly to wish only to be wise.

232.—Whatever pretext we give to our afflictions it is always interest or vanity that causes them.

233.—In afflictions there are various kinds of hypocrisy. In one, under the pretext of weeping for one dear to us we bemoan ourselves; we regret her good opinion of us, we deplore the loss of our comfort, our pleasure, our consideration. Thus the dead have the credit of tears shed for the living. I affirm it is a kind of hypocrisy which in these afflictions deceives itself. There is another kind not so innocent because it imposes on all the world, that is the grief of those who aspire to the glory of a noble and immortal sorrow. After Time, which absorbs all, has obliterated what sorrow they had, they still obstinately obtrude their tears, their sighs their groans, they wear a solemn face, and try to persuade others by all their acts, that their grief will end only with their life. This sad and distressing vanity is commonly found in ambitious women. As their sex closes to them all paths to glory, they strive to render themselves celebrated by showing an inconsolable affliction. There is yet another kind of tears arising from but small sources, which flow easily and cease as easily. One weeps to achieve a reputation for tenderness, weeps to be pitied, weeps to be bewept, in fact one weeps to avoid the disgrace of not weeping!

234.—It is more often from pride than from ignorance that we are so obstinately opposed to current opinions; we find the first places taken, and we do not want to be the last.

235.—We are easily consoled at the misfortunes of our friends when they enable us to prove our tenderness for them.

236.—It would seem that even self-love may be the dupe of goodness and forget itself when we work for others. And yet it is but taking the shortest way to arrive at its aim, taking usury under the pretext of giving, in fact winning everybody in a subtle and delicate manner.

237.—No one should be praised for his goodness if he has not strength enough to be wicked. All other goodness is but too often an idleness or powerlessness of will.

238.—It is not so dangerous to do wrong to most men, as to do them too much good.

239.—Nothing flatters our pride so much as the confidence of the great, because we regard it as the result of our worth, without remembering that generally it is but vanity, or the inability to keep a secret.

240.—We may say of conformity as distinguished from beauty, that it is a symmetry which knows no rules, and a secret harmony of features both one with each other and with the colour and appearance of the person.

241.—Flirtation is at the bottom of woman's nature, although all do not practise it, some being restrained by fear, others by sense.

242.—We often bore others when we think we cannot possibly bore them.

243.—Few things are impossible in themselves; application to make them succeed fails us more often than the means.

244.—Sovereign ability consists in knowing the value of things.

245.—There is great ability in knowing how to conceal one's ability.

246.—What seems generosity is often disguised ambition, that despises small to run after greater interest.

247.—The fidelity of most men is merely an invention of self-love to win confidence; a method to place us above others and to render us depositaries of the most important matters.

248.—Magnanimity despises all, to win all.

249.—There is no less eloquence in the voice, in the eyes and in the air of a speaker than in his choice of words.

250.—True eloquence consists in saying all that should be, not all that could be said.

251.—There are people whose faults become them, others whose very virtues disgrace them.

252.—It is as common to change one's tastes, as it is uncommon to change one's inclinations.

253.—Interest sets at work all sorts of virtues and vices.

254.—Humility is often a feigned submission which we employ to supplant others. It is one of the devices of Pride to lower us to raise us; and truly pride transforms itself in a thousand ways, and is never so well disguised and more able to deceive than when it hides itself under the form of humility.

255.—All feelings have their peculiar tone of voice, gestures and looks, and this harmony, as it is good or bad, pleasant or unpleasant, makes people agreeable or disagreeable.

256.—In all professions we affect a part and an appearance to seem what we wish to be. Thus the world is merely composed of actors.

257.—Gravity is a mysterious carriage of the body invented to conceal the want of mind.

258.—Good taste arises more from judgment than wit.

259.—The pleasure of love is in loving, we are happier in the passion we feel than in that we inspire.

260.—Civility is but a desire to receive civility, and to be esteemed polite.

261.—The usual education of young people is to inspire them with a second self-love.

262.—There is no passion wherein self-love reigns so powerfully as in love, and one is always more ready to sacrifice the peace of the loved one than his own.

263.—What we call liberality is often but the vanity of giving, which we like more than that we give away.

264.—Pity is often a reflection of our own evils in the ills of others. It is a delicate foresight of the troubles into which we may fall. We help others that on like occasions we may be helped ourselves, and these services which we render, are in reality benefits we confer on ourselves by anticipation.

265.—A narrow mind begets obstinacy, and we do not easily believe what we cannot see.

266.—We deceive ourselves if we believe that there are violent passions like ambition and love that can triumph over others. Idleness, languishing as she is, does not often fail in being mistress; she usurps authority over all the plans and actions of life; imperceptibly consuming and destroying both passions and virtues.

267.—A quickness in believing evil without having sufficiently examined it, is the effect of pride and laziness. We wish to find the guilty, and we do not wish to trouble ourselves in examining the crime.

268.—We credit judges with the meanest motives, and yet we desire our reputation and fame should depend upon the judgment of men, who are all, either from their jealousy or pre-occupation or want of intelligence, opposed to us—and yet it is only to make these men decide in our favour that we peril in so many ways both our peace and our life.

269.—No man is clever enough to know all the evil he does.

270.—One honour won is a surety for more.

271.—Youth is a continual intoxication; it is the fever of reason.

272.—Nothing should so humiliate men who have deserved great praise, as the care they have taken to acquire it by the smallest means.

273.—There are persons of whom the world approves who have no merit beyond the vices they use in the affairs of life.

274.—The beauty of novelty is to love as the flower to the fruit; it lends a lustre which is easily lost, but which never returns.

275.—Natural goodness, which boasts of being so apparent, is often smothered by the least interest.

276.—Absence extinguishes small passions and increases great ones, as the wind will blow out a candle, and blow in a fire.

277.—Women often think they love when they do not love. The business of a love affair, the emotion of mind that sentiment induces, the natural bias towards the pleasure of being loved, the difficulty of refusing, persuades them that they have real passion when they have but flirtation.

278.—What makes us so often discontented with those who transact business for us is that they almost always abandon the interest of their friends for the interest of the business, because they wish to have the honour of succeeding in that which they have undertaken.

279.—When we exaggerate the tenderness of our friends towards us, it is often less from gratitude than from a desire to exhibit our own merit.

280.—The praise we give to new comers into the world arises from the envy we bear to those who are established.

281.—Pride, which inspires, often serves to moderate envy.

282.—Some disguised lies so resemble truth, that we should judge badly were we not deceived.

283.—Sometimes there is not less ability in knowing how to use than in giving good advice.

284.—There are wicked people who would be much less dangerous if they were wholly without goodness.

285.—Magnanimity is sufficiently defined by its name, nevertheless one can say it is the good sense of pride, the most noble way of receiving praise.

286.—It is impossible to love a second time those whom we have really ceased to love.

287.—Fertility of mind does not furnish us with so many resources on the same matter, as the lack of intelligence makes us hesitate at each thing our imagination presents, and hinders us from at first discerning which is the best.

288.—There are matters and maladies which at certain times remedies only serve to make worse; true skill consists in knowing when it is dangerous to use them.

289.—Affected simplicity is refined imposture.

290.—There are as many errors of temper as of mind.

291.—Man's merit, like the crops, has its season.

292.—One may say of temper as of many buildings; it has divers aspects, some agreeable, others disagreeable.

293.—Moderation cannot claim the merit of opposing and overcoming Ambition: they are never found together. Moderation is the languor and sloth of the soul, Ambition its activity and heat.

294.—We always like those who admire us, we do not always like those whom we admire.

295.—It is well that we know not all our wishes.

296.—It is difficult to love those we do not esteem, but it is no less so to love those whom we esteem much more than ourselves.

297.—Bodily temperaments have a common course and rule which imperceptibly affect our will. They advance in combination, and successively exercise a secret empire over us, so that, without our perceiving it, they become a great part of all our actions.

298.—The gratitude of most men is but a secret desire of receiving greater benefits.

299.—Almost all the world takes pleasure in paying small debts; many people show gratitude for trifling, but there is hardly one who does not show ingratitude for great favours.

300.—There are follies as catching as infections.

301.—Many people despise, but few know how to bestow wealth.

302.—Only in things of small value we usually are bold enough not to trust to appearances.

303.—Whatever good quality may be imputed to us, we ourselves find nothing new in it.

304.—We may forgive those who bore us, we cannot forgive those whom we bore.

305.—Interest which is accused of all our misdeeds often should be praised for our good deeds.

306.—We find very few ungrateful people when we are able to confer favours.

307.—It is as proper to be boastful alone as it is ridiculous to be so in company.

308.—Moderation is made a virtue to limit the ambition of the great; to console ordinary people for their small fortune and equally small ability.

309.—There are persons fated to be fools, who commit follies not only by choice, but who are forced by fortune to do so.

310.—Sometimes there are accidents in our life the skilful extrication from which demands a little folly.

311.—If there be men whose folly has never appeared, it is because it has never been closely looked for.

312.—Lovers are never tired of each other,—they always speak of themselves.

313.—How is it that our memory is good enough to retain the least triviality that happens to us, and yet not good enough to recollect how often we have told it to the same person?

314.—The extreme delight we take in talking of ourselves should warn us that it is not shared by those who listen.

315.—What commonly hinders us from showing the recesses of our heart to our friends, is not the distrust we have of them, but that we have of ourselves.

316.—Weak persons cannot be sincere.

317.—It is a small misfortune to oblige an ungrateful man; but it is unbearable to be obliged by a scoundrel.

318.—We may find means to cure a fool of his folly, but there are none to set straight a cross-grained spirit.

319.—If we take the liberty to dwell on their faults we cannot long preserve the feelings we should hold towards our friends and benefactors.

320.—To praise princes for virtues they do not possess is but to reproach them with impunity.

321.—We are nearer loving those who hate us, than those who love us more than we desire.

322.—Those only are despicable who fear to be despised.

323.—Our wisdom is no less at the mercy of Fortune than our goods.

324.—There is more self-love than love in jealousy.

325.—We often comfort ourselves by the weakness of evils, for which reason has not the strength to console us.

326.—Ridicule dishonours more than dishonour itself.

327.—We own to small faults to persuade others that we have not great ones.

328.—Envy is more irreconcilable than hatred.

329.—We believe, sometimes, that we hate flattery —we only dislike the method.

330.—We pardon in the degree that we love.

331.—It is more difficult to be faithful to a mistress when one is happy, than when we are ill-treated by her.

332.—Women do not know all their powers of flirtation.

333.—Women cannot be completely severe unless they hate.

334.—Women can less easily resign flirtations than love.

335.—In love deceit almost always goes further than mistrust.

336.—There is a kind of love, the excess of which forbids jealousy.

337.—There are certain good qualities as there are senses, and those who want them can neither perceive nor understand them.

338.—When our hatred is too bitter it places us below those whom we hate.

339.—We only appreciate our good or evil in proportion to our self-love.

340.—The wit of most women rather strengthens their folly than their reason.

341.—The heat of youth is not more opposed to safety than the coldness of age.

342.—The accent of our native country dwells in the heart and mind as well as on the tongue.

343.—To be a great man one should know how to profit by every phase of fortune.

344.—Most men, like plants, possess hidden qualities which chance discovers.

345.—Opportunity makes us known to others, but more to ourselves.

346.—If a woman's temper is beyond control there can be no control of the mind or heart.

347.—We hardly find any persons of good sense, save those who agree with us.

348.—When one loves one doubts even what one most believes.

349.—The greatest miracle of love is to eradicate flirtation.

350.—Why we hate with so much bitterness those who deceive us is because they think themselves more clever than we are.

351.—We have much trouble to break with one, when we no longer are in love.

352.—We almost always are bored with persons with whom we should not be bored.

353.—A gentleman may love like a lunatic, but not like a beast.

354.—There are certain defects which well mounted glitter like virtue itself.

355.—Sometimes we lose friends for whose loss our regret is greater than our grief, and others for whom our grief is greater than our regret.

356.—Usually we only praise heartily those who admire us.

357.—Little minds are too much wounded by little things; great minds see all and are not even hurt.

358.—Humility is the true proof of Christian virtues; without it we retain all our faults, and they are only covered by pride to hide them from others, and often from ourselves.

359.—Infidelities should extinguish love, and we ought not to be jealous when we have cause to be so. No persons escape causing jealousy who are worthy of exciting it.

360.—We are more humiliated by the least infidelity towards us, than by our greatest towards others.

361.—Jealousy is always born with love, but does not always die with it.

362.—Most women do not grieve so much for the death of their lovers for love's-sake, as to show they were worthy of being beloved.

363.—The evils we do to others give us less pain than those we do to ourselves.

364.—We well know that it is bad taste to talk of our wives; but we do not so well know that it is the same to speak of ourselves.

365.—There are virtues which degenerate into vices when they arise from Nature, and others which when acquired are never perfect. For example, reason must teach us to manage our estate and our confidence, while Nature should have given us goodness and valour.

366.—However we distrust the sincerity of those whom we talk with, we always believe them more sincere with us than with others.

367.—There are few virtuous women who are not tired of their part.

368.—The greater number of good women are like concealed treasures, safe as no one has searched for them.

369.—The violences we put upon ourselves to escape love are often more cruel than the cruelty of those we love.

370.—There are not many cowards who know the whole of their fear.

371.—It is generally the fault of the loved one not to perceive when love ceases.

372.—Most young people think they are natural when they are only boorish and rude.

373.—Some tears after having deceived others deceive ourselves.

374.—If we think we love a woman for love of herself we are greatly deceived.

375.—Ordinary men commonly condemn what is beyond them.

376.—Envy is destroyed by true friendship, flirtation by true love.

377.—The greatest mistake of penetration is not to have fallen short, but to have gone too far.

378.—We may bestow advice, but we cannot inspire the conduct.

379.—As our merit declines so also does our taste.

380.—Fortune makes visible our virtues or our vices, as light does objects.

381.—The struggle we undergo to remain faithful to one we love is little better than infidelity.

382.—Our actions are like the rhymed ends of blank verses (*Bouts-Rimés*) where to each one puts what construction he pleases.

383.—The desire of talking about ourselves, and of putting our faults in the light we wish them to be seen, forms a great part of our sincerity.

384.—We should only be astonished at still being able to be astonished.

385.—It is equally as difficult to be contented when one has too much or too little love.

386.—No people are more often wrong than those who will not allow themselves to be wrong.

387.—A fool has not stuff in him to be good.

388.—If vanity does not overthrow all virtues, at least she makes them totter.

389.—What makes the vanity of others unsupportable is that it wounds our own.

390.—We give up more easily our interest than our taste.

391.—Fortune appears so blind to none as to those to whom she has done no good.

392.—We should manage fortune like our health, enjoy it when it is good, be patient when it is bad, and never resort to strong remedies but in an extremity.

393.—Awkwardness sometimes disappears in the camp, never in the court.

394.—A man is often more clever than one other, but not than all others.

395.—We are often less unhappy at being deceived by one we loved, than on being deceived.

396.—We keep our first lover for a long time—if we do not get a second.

397.—We have not the courage to say generally that we have no faults, and that our enemies have no good qualities; but in fact we are not far from believing so.

398.—Of all our faults that which we most readily admit is idleness: we believe that it makes all virtues ineffectual, and that without utterly destroying, it at least suspends their operation.

399.—There is a kind of greatness which does not depend upon fortune: it is a certain manner what distinguishes us, and which seems to destine us for great things; it is the value we insensibly set upon ourselves; it is by this quality that we gain the deference of other men, and it is this which commonly raises us more above them, than birth, rank, or even merit itself.

400.—There may be talent without position, but there is no position without some kind of talent.

401.—Rank is to merit what dress is to a pretty woman.

402.—What we find the least of in flirtation is love.

403.—Fortune sometimes uses our faults to exalt us, and there are tiresome people whose deserts would be ill rewarded if we did not desire to purchase their absence.

404.—It appears that nature has hid at the bottom of our hearts talents and abilities unknown to us. It is only the passions that have the power of bringing them to light, and sometimes give us views more true and more perfect than art could possibly do.

405.—We reach quite inexperienced the different stages of life, and often, in spite of the number of our years, we lack experience.

406.—Flirts make it a point of honour to be jealous of their lovers, to conceal their envy of other women.

407.—It may well be that those who have trapped us by their tricks do not seem to us so foolish as we seem to ourselves when trapped by the tricks of others.

408.—The most dangerous folly of old persons who have been loveable is to forget that they are no longer so.

409.—We should often be ashamed of our very best actions if the world only saw the motives which caused them.

410.—The greatest effort of friendship is not to show our faults to a friend, but to show him his own.

411.—We have few faults which are not far more excusable than the means we adopt to hide them.

412.—Whatever disgrace we may have deserved, it is almost always in our power to re-establish our character.

413.—A man cannot please long who has only one kind of wit.

414.—Idiots and lunatics see only their own wit.

415.—Wit sometimes enables us to act rudely with impunity.

416.—The vivacity which increases in old age is not far removed from folly.

417.—In love the quickest is always the best cure.

418.—Young women who do not want to appear flirts, and old men who do not want to appear ridiculous, should not talk of love as a matter wherein they can have any interest.

419.—We may seem great in a post beneath our capacity, but we oftener seem little in a post above it.

420.—We often believe we have constancy in misfortune when we have nothing but debasement, and we suffer misfortunes without regarding them as cowards who let themselves be killed from fear of defending themselves.

421.—Conceit causes more conversation than wit.

422.—All passions make us commit some faults, love alone makes us ridiculous.

423.—Few know how to be old.

424.—We often credit ourselves with vices the reverse of what we have, thus when weak we boast of our obstinacy.

425.—Penetration has a spice of divination in it which tickles our vanity more than any other quality of the mind.

426.—The charm of novelty and old custom, however opposite to each other, equally blind us to the faults of our friends.

427.—Most friends sicken us of friendship, most devotees of devotion.

428.—We easily forgive in our friends those faults we do not perceive.

429.—Women who love, pardon more readily great indiscretions than little infidelities.

430.—In the old age of love as in life we still survive for the evils, though no longer for the pleasures.

431.—Nothing prevents our being unaffected so much as our desire to seem so.

432.—To praise good actions heartily is in some measure to take part in them.

433.—The most certain sign of being born with great qualities is to be born without envy.

434.—When our friends have deceived us we owe them but indifference to the tokens of their friendship, yet for their misfortunes we always owe them pity.

435.—Luck and temper rule the world.

436.—It is far easier to know men than to know man.

437.—We should not judge of a man's merit by his great abilities, but by the use he makes of them.

438.—There is a certain lively gratitude which not only releases us from benefits received, but which also, by making a return to our friends as payment, renders them indebted to us.

439.—We should earnestly desire but few things if we clearly knew what we desired.

440.—The cause why the majority of women are so little given to friendship is, that it is insipid after having felt love.

441.—As in friendship so in love, we are often happier from ignorance than from knowledge.

442.—We try to make a virtue of vices we are loth to correct.

443.—The most violent passions give some respite, but vanity always disturbs us.

444.—Old fools are more foolish than young fools.

445.—Weakness is more hostile to virtue than vice.

446.—What makes the grief of shame and jealousy so acute is that vanity cannot aid us in enduring them.

447.—Propriety is the least of all laws, but the most obeyed.

448.—A well-trained mind has less difficulty in submitting to than in guiding an ill-trained mind.

449.—When fortune surprises us by giving us some great office without having gradually led us to expect it, or without having raised our hopes, it is well nigh impossible to occupy it well, and to appear worthy to fill it.

450.—Our pride is often increased by what we retrench from our other faults.

451.—No fools so wearisome as those who have some wit.

452.—No one believes that in every respect he is behind the man he considers the ablest in the world.

453.—In great matters we should not try so much to create opportunities as to utilise those that offer themselves.

454.—There are few occasions when we should make a bad bargain by giving up the good on condition that no ill was said of us.

455.—However disposed the world may be to judge wrongly, it far oftener favours false merit than does justice to true.

456.—Sometimes we meet a fool with wit, never one with discretion.

457.—We should gain more by letting the world see what we are than by trying to seem what we are not.

458.—Our enemies come nearer the truth in the opinions they form of us than we do in our opinion of ourselves.

459.—There are many remedies to cure love, yet none are infallible.

460.—It would be well for us if we knew all our passions make us do.

461.—Age is a tyrant who forbids at the penalty of life all the pleasures of youth.

462.—The same pride which makes us blame faults from which we believe ourselves free causes us to despise the good qualities we have not.

463.—There is often more pride than goodness in our grief for our enemies' miseries; it is to show how superior we are to them, that we bestow on them the sign of our compassion.

464.—There exists an excess of good and evil which surpasses our comprehension.

465.—Innocence is most fortunate if it finds the same protection as crime.

466.—Of all the violent passions the one that becomes a woman best is love.

467.—Vanity makes us sin more against our taste than reason.

468.—Some bad qualities form great talents.

469.—We never desire earnestly what we desire in reason.

470.—All our qualities are uncertain and doubtful, both the good as well as the bad, and nearly all are creatures of opportunities.

471.—In their first passion women love their lovers, in all the others they love love.

472.—Pride as the other passions has its follies. We are ashamed to own we are jealous, and yet we plume ourselves in having been and being able to be so.

473.—However rare true love is, true friendship is rarer.

474.—There are few women whose charm survives their beauty.

475.—The desire to be pitied or to be admired often forms the greater part of our confidence.

476.—Our envy always lasts longer than the happiness of those we envy.

477.—The same firmness that enables us to resist love enables us to make our resistance durable and lasting. So weak persons who are always excited by passions are seldom really possessed of any.

478.—Fancy does not enable us to invent so many different contradictions as there are by nature in every heart.

479.—It is only people who possess firmness who can possess true gentleness. In those who appear gentle it is generally only weakness, which is readily converted into harshness.

480.—Timidity is a fault which is dangerous to blame in those we desire to cure of it.

481.—Nothing is rarer than true good nature, those who think they have it are generally only pliant or weak.

482.—The mind attaches itself by idleness and habit to whatever is easy or pleasant. This habit always places bounds to our knowledge, and no one has ever yet taken the pains to enlarge and expand his mind to the full extent of its capacities.

483.—Usually we are more satirical from vanity than malice.

484.—When the heart is still disturbed by the relics of a passion it is proner to take up a new one than when wholly cured.

485.—Those who have had great passions often find all their lives made miserable in being cured of them.

486.—More persons exist without self-love than without envy.

487.—We have more idleness in the mind than in the body.

488.—The calm or disturbance of our mind does not depend so much on what we regard as the more important things of life, as in a judicious or injudicious arrangement of the little things of daily occurrence.

489.—However wicked men may be, they do not dare openly to appear the enemies of virtue, and when they desire to persecute her they either pretend to believe her false or attribute crimes to her.

490.—We often go from love to ambition, but we never return from ambition to love.

491.—Extreme avarice is nearly always mistaken, there is no passion which is oftener further away from its mark, nor upon which the present has so much power to the prejudice of the future.

492.—Avarice often produces opposite results: there are an infinite number of persons who sacrifice their property to doubtful and distant expectations, others mistake great future advantages for small present interests.

493.—It appears that men do not find they have enough faults, as they increase the number by certain peculiar qualities that they affect to assume, and which they cultivate with so great assiduity that at length they become natural faults, which they can no longer correct.

494.—What makes us see that men know their faults better than we imagine, is that they are never wrong when they speak of their conduct; the same self-love that usually blinds them enlightens them, and gives them such true views as to make them suppress or disguise the smallest thing that might be censured.

495.—Young men entering life should be either shy or bold; a solemn and sedate manner usually degenerates into impertinence.

496.—Quarrels would not last long if the fault was only on one side.

497.—It is valueless to a woman to be young unless pretty, or to be pretty unless young.

498.—Some persons are so frivolous and fickle that they are as far removed from real defects as from substantial qualities.

499.—We do not usually reckon a woman's first flirtation until she has had a second.

500.—Some people are so self-occupied that when in love they find a mode by which to be engrossed with the passion without being so with the person they love.

501.—Love, though so very agreeable, pleases more by its ways than by itself.

502.—A little wit with good sense bores less in the long run than much wit with ill nature.

503.—Jealousy is the worst of all evils, yet the one that is least pitied by those who cause it.

504.—Thus having treated of the hollowness of so many apparent virtues, it is but just to say something on the hollowness of the contempt for death. I allude to that contempt of death which the heathen boasted they derived from their unaided understanding, without the hope of a future state. There is a difference between meeting death with courage and despising it. The first is common enough, the last I think always feigned. Yet everything that could be has been written to persuade us that death is no evil, and the weakest of men, equally with the bravest, have given many noble examples on which to found such an opinion, still I do not think that any man of good sense has ever yet believed in it. And the pains we take to persuade others as well as ourselves amply show that the task is far from easy. For many reasons we may be disgusted with life, but for none may we despise it. Not even those who commit suicide regard it as a light matter, and are as much alarmed and startled as the rest of the world if death meets them in a different way than the one they have selected. The difference we observe in the courage of so great a number of brave men, is from meeting death in a way different from what they imagined, when it shows itself nearer at one time than at another. Thus it ultimately happens that having despised death when they were ignorant of it, they dread it when they become acquainted with it. If we could avoid seeing it with all its surroundings, we might perhaps believe that it was not the greatest of evils. The wisest and bravest are those who take the best means to avoid reflecting on it, as every man who sees it in its real light regards it as dreadful. The necessity of dying created all the constancy of philosophers. They thought it but right to go with a good grace when they could not avoid going, and being unable to prolong their lives indefinitely, nothing remained but to build an immortal reputation, and to save from the general wreck all that could be saved. To put a good face upon it, let it suffice, not to say all that we think to ourselves, but rely more on our nature than on our fallible reason, which might make us think we could approach death with indifference. The glory of dying with courage, the hope of being regretted, the desire to leave behind us a good reputation, the assurance of being enfranchised from the miseries of life and being no longer dependent on the wiles of fortune, are resources which should not be passed over. But we must not regard them as infallible. They should affect us in the same proportion as a single shelter affects those who in war storm a fortress. At a distance they think it may afford cover, but when near they find it only a feeble protection. It is only deceiving ourselves to imagine that death, when near, will seem the same as at a distance, or that our feelings, which are merely weaknesses, are naturally so strong that they will not suffer in an attack of the rudest of trials. It is equally as absurd to try the effect of self-esteem and to think it will enable us to count as naught what will of necessity destroy it. And the mind in which we trust to find so many resources will be far too weak in the struggle to persuade us in the way we wish. For it is this which betrays us so frequently, and which, instead of filling us with contempt of death, serves but to show us all that is frightful and fearful. The most it can do for us is to persuade us to avert our gaze and fix it on other objects. Cato and Brutus each selected noble ones. A lackey sometime ago contented himself by dancing on the scaffold when he was about to be broken on the wheel. So however diverse the motives they but realize the same result. For the rest it is a fact that whatever difference there may be between the peer and the peasant, we have constantly seen both the one and the other meet death with the same composure. Still there is always this difference, that the contempt the peer shows for death is but the love of fame which hides death from his sight; in the peasant it is but the result of his limited vision that hides from him the extent of the evil, end leaves him free to reflect on other things.

THE FIRST SUPPLEMENT

The following reflections are extracted from the first two editions of La Rochefoucauld, having been suppressed by the author in succeeding issues.

I.—Self-love is the love *of* self, and of all things *for* self. It makes men self-worshippers, and if fortune permits them, causes them to tyrannize over others; it is never quiet when out of itself, and only rests upon other subjects as a bee upon flowers, to extract from them its proper food. Nothing is so headstrong as its desires, nothing so well concealed as its designs, nothing so skilful as its management; its suppleness is beyond description; its changes surpass those of the metamorphoses, its refinements those of chemistry. We can neither plumb the depths nor pierce the shades of its recesses. Therein it is hidden from the most far-seeing eyes, therein it takes a thousand imperceptible folds. There it is often to itself invisible; it there conceives, there nourishes and rears, without being aware of it, numberless loves and hatreds, some so monstrous that when they are brought to light it disowns them, and cannot resolve to avow them. In the night which covers it are born the ridiculous persuasions it has of itself, thence come its errors, its ignorance, its silly mistakes; thence it is led to believe that its passions which sleep are dead, and to think that it has lost all appetite for that of which it is sated. But this thick darkness which conceals it from itself does not hinder it from seeing that perfectly which is out of itself; and in this it resembles our eyes which behold all, and yet cannot set their own forms. In fact, in great concerns and important matters when the violence of its desires summons all its attention, it sees, feels, hears, imagines, suspects, penetrates, divines all: so that we might think that each of its passions had a magic power proper to it. Nothing is so close and strong as its attachments, which, in sight of the extreme misfortunes which threaten it, it vainly attempts to break. Yet sometimes it effects that without trouble and quickly, which it failed to do with its whole power and in the course of years, whence we may fairly conclude that it is by itself that its desires are inflamed, rather than by the beauty and merit of its objects, that its own taste embellishes and heightens them; that it is itself the game it pursues, and that it follows eagerly when it runs after that upon which itself is eager. It is made up of contraries. It is imperious and obedient, sincere and false, piteous and cruel, timid and bold. It has different desires according to the diversity of temperaments, which turn and fix it sometimes upon riches, sometimes on pleasures. It changes according to our age, our fortunes, and our hopes; it is quite indifferent whether it has many or one, because it can split itself into many portions, and unite in one as it pleases. It is inconstant, and besides the changes which arise from strange causes it has an infinity born of itself, and of its own substance. It is inconstant through inconstancy, of lightness, love, novelty, lassitude and distaste. It is capricious, and one sees it sometimes work with intense eagerness and with incredible labour to obtain things of little use to it which are even hurtful, but which it pursues because it wishes for them. It is silly, and often throws its whole application on the utmost frivolities. It finds all its pleasure in the dullest matters, and places its pride in the most contemptible. It is seen in all states of life, and in all conditions; it lives everywhere and upon everything; it subsists on nothing; it accommodates itself either to things or to the want of them; it goes over to those who are at war with it, enters into their designs, and, this is wonderful, it, with them, hates even itself; it conspires for its own loss, it works towards its own ruin—in fact, caring only to exist, and providing that it may *be*, it will be its own enemy! We must therefore not be surprised if it is sometimes united to the rudest austerity, and if it enters so boldly into partnership to destroy her, because when it is rooted out in one place it re-establishes itself in another. When it fancies that it abandons its pleasure it merely changes or suspends its enjoyment. When even it is conquered in its full flight, we find that it triumphs in its own defeat. Here then is the picture of self-love whereof the whole of our life is but one long agitation. The sea is its living image; and in the flux and reflux of its continuous waves there is a faithful expression of the stormy succession of its thoughts and of its eternal motion. (Edition of 1665, No. 1.)

II.—Passions are only the different degrees of the heat or coldness of the blood. (1665, No. 13.)

III.—Moderation in good fortune is but apprehension of the shame which follows upon haughtiness, or a fear of losing what we have. (1665, No. 18.)

IV.—Moderation is like temperance in eating; we could eat more but we fear to make ourselves ill. (1665, No. 21.)

V.—Everybody finds that to abuse in another which he finds worthy of abuse in himself. (1665, No. 33.)

VI.—Pride, as if tired of its artifices and its different metamorphoses, after having solely filled the divers parts of the comedy of life, exhibits itself with its natural face, and is discovered by haughtiness; so much so that we may truly say that haughtiness is but the flash and open declaration of pride. (1665, No. 37.)

VII.—One kind of happiness is to know exactly at what point to be miserable. (1665, No. 53.)

VIII.—When we do not find peace of mind in ourselves it is useless to seek it elsewhere. (1665, No. 53.)

IX.—One should be able to answer for one's fortune, so as to be able to answer for what we shall do. (1665, No. 70.)

X.—Love is to the soul of him who loves, what the soul is to the body which it animates. (1665, No. 77.)

XI.—As one is never at liberty to love or to cease from loving, the lover cannot with justice complain of the inconstancy of his mistress, nor she of the fickleness of her lover. (1665, No. 81.)

XII.—Justice in those judges who are moderate is but a love of their place. (1665, No. 89.)

XIII.—When we are tired of loving we are quite content if our mistress should become faithless, to loose us from our fidelity. (1665, No. 85.)

XIV.—The first impulse of joy which we feel at the happiness of our friends arises neither from our natural goodness nor from friendship; it is the result of self-love, which flatters us with being lucky in our own turn, or in reaping something from the good fortune of our friends. (1665, No. 97.)

XV.—In the adversity of our best friends we always find something which is not wholly displeasing to us. (1665, No. 99.)

XVI.—How shall we hope that another person will keep our secret if we do not keep it ourselves. (1665, No. 100.)

XVII.—As if it was not sufficient that self-love should have the power to change itself, it has added that of changing other objects, and this it does in a very astonishing manner; for not only does it so well disguise them that it is itself deceived, but it even changes the state and nature of things. Thus, when a female is adverse to us, and she turns her hate and persecution against us, self-love pronounces on her actions with all the severity of justice; it exaggerates the faults till they are enormous, and looks at her good qualities in so disadvantageous a light that they become more displeasing than her faults. If however the same female becomes favourable to us, or certain of our interests reconcile her to us, our sole self interest gives her back the lustre which our hatred deprived her of. The bad qualities become effaced, the good ones appear with a redoubled advantage; we even summon all our indulgence to justify the war she has made upon us. Now although all passions prove this truth, that of love exhibits it most clearly; for we may see a lover moved with rage by the neglect or the infidelity of her whom he loves, and meditating the utmost vengeance that his passion can inspire. Nevertheless as soon as the sight of his beloved has calmed the fury of his movements, his passion holds that beauty innocent; he only accuses himself, he condemns his condemnations, and by the miraculous power of self-love, he whitens the blackest actions of his mistress, and takes from her all crime to lay it on himself. (No date or number is given for this maxim.)

XVIII.—There are none who press so heavily on others as the lazy ones, when they have satisfied their idleness, and wish to appear industrious. (1666, No. 91.)

XIX.—The blindness of men is the most dangerous effect of their pride; it seems to nourish and augment it, it deprives us of knowledge of remedies which can solace our miseries and can cure our faults. (1665, No. 102.)

XX.—One has never less reason than when one despairs of finding it in others. (1665, No. 103.)

XXI.—Philosophers, and Seneca above all, have not diminished crimes by their precepts; they have only used them in the building up of pride. (1665, No. 105.)

XXII.—It is a proof of little friendship not to perceive the growing coolness of that of our friends. (1666, No. 97.)

XXIII.—The most wise may be so in indifferent and ordinary matters, but they are seldom so in their most serious affairs. (1665, No. 132.)

XXIV.—The most subtle folly grows out of the most subtle wisdom. (1665, No. 134.)

XXV.—Sobriety is the love of health, or an incapacity to eat much. (1665, No. 135.)

XXVI.—We never forget things so well as when we are tired of talking of them. (1665, No. 144.)

XXVII.—The praise bestowed upon us is at least useful in rooting us in the practice of virtue. (1665, No. 155.)

XXVIII.—Self-love takes care to prevent him whom we flatter from being him who most flatters us. (1665, No. 157.)

XXIX.—Men only blame vice and praise virtue from interest. (1665, No. 151.)

XXX.—We make no difference in the kinds of anger, although there is that which is light and almost innocent, which arises from warmth of complexion, temperament, and another very criminal, which is, to speak properly, the fury of pride. (1665, No. 159.)

XXXI.—Great souls are not those who have fewer passions and more virtues than the common, but those only who have greater designs. (1665, No. 161.)

XXXII.—Kings do with men as with pieces of money; they make them bear what value they will, and one is forced to receive them according to their currency value, and not at their true worth. (1665, No. 165.)

XXXIII.—Natural ferocity makes fewer people cruel than self-love. (1665, No. 174.)

XXXIV.—One may say of all our virtues as an Italian poet says of the propriety of women, that it is often merely the art of appearing chaste. (1665, No. 176.)

XXXV.—There are crimes which become innocent and even glorious by their brilliancy, their number, or their excess; thus it happens that public robbery is called financial skill, and the unjust capture of provinces is called a conquest. (1665, No. 192.)

XXXVI.—One never finds in man good or evil in excess. (1665, No. 201.)

XXXVII.—Those who are incapable of committing great crimes do not easily suspect others. (1665, No. 208.)

XXXVIII.—The pomp of funerals concerns rather the vanity of the living, than the honour of the dead. (1665, No. 213.)

XXXIX.—Whatever variety and change appears in the world, we may remark a secret chain, and a regulated order of all time by Providence, which makes everything follow in due rank and fall into its destined course. (1665, No. 225.)

XL.—Intrepidity should sustain the heart in conspiracies in place of valour which alone furnishes all the firmness which is necessary for the perils of war. (1665, No. 231.)

XLI.—Those who wish to define victory by her birth will be tempted to imitate the poets, and to call her the Daughter of Heaven, since they cannot find her origin on earth. Truly she is produced from an infinity of actions, which instead of wishing to beget her, only look to the particular interests of their masters, since all those who compose an army, in aiming at their own rise and glory, produce a good so great and general. (1665, No. 232.)

XLII.—That man who has never been in danger cannot answer for his courage. (1665, No. 236.)

XLIII.—We more often place bounds on our gratitude than on our desires and our hopes. (1665, No. 241.)

XLIV.—Imitation is always unhappy, for all which is counterfeit displeases by the very things which charm us when they are original (*Naturelles*). (1665, No. 245.)

XLV.—We do not regret the loss of our friends according to *their* merits, but according to OUR wants, and the opinion with which we believed we had impressed them of our worth. (1665, No. 248.)

XLVI.—It is very hard to separate the general goodness spread all over the world from great cleverness. (1665, No. 252.)

XLVII.—For us to be always good, others should believe that they cannot behave wickedly to us with impunity. (1665, No. 254.)

XLVIII.—A confidence in being able to please is often an infallible means of being displeasing. (1665, No. 256.)

XLIX.—The confidence we have in ourselves arises in a great measure from that that we have in others. (1665, No. 258.)

L.—There is a general revolution which changes the tastes of the mind as well as the fortunes of the world. (1665, No. 250.)

LI.—Truth is foundation and the reason of the perfection of beauty, for of whatever stature a thing may be, it cannot be beautiful and perfect unless it be truly that she should be, and possess truly all that she should have (1665, No. 260.)

LII.—There are fine things which are more brilliant when unfinished than when finished too much. (1665, No. 262.)

LIII.—Magnanimity is a noble effort of pride which makes a man master of himself, to make him master of all things. (1665, No. 271.)

LIV.—Luxury and too refined a policy in states are a sure presage of their fall, because all parties looking after their own interest turn away from the public good. (1665, No. 282.)

LV.—Of all passions that which is least known to us is idleness; she is the most ardent and evil of all, although her violence may be insensible, and the evils she causes concealed; if we consider her power attentively we shall find that in all encounters she makes herself mistress of our sentiments, our interests, and our pleasures; like the (fabled) Remora, she can stop the greatest vessels, she is a hidden rock, more dangerous in the most important matters than sudden squalls and the most violent tempests. The repose of idleness is a magic charm which suddenly suspends the most ardent pursuits and the most obstinate resolutions. In fact to give a true notion of this passion we must add that idleness, like a beatitude of the soul, consoles us for all losses and fills the vacancy of all our wants. (1665, No. 290.)

LVI.—We are very fond of reading others' characters, but we do not like to be read ourselves. (1665, No. 296.)

LVII.—What a tiresome malady is that which forces one to preserve your health by a severe regimen. (1665, No. 298.)

LVIII.—It is much easier to take love when one is free, than to get rid of it after having taken it. (1665, No. 300.)

LIX.—Women for the most part surrender themselves more from weakness than from passion. Whence it is that bold and pushing men succeed better than others, although they are not so lovable. (1665, No. 301.)

LX.—Not to love is in love, an infallible means of being beloved. (1665, No. 302.)

LXI.—The sincerity which lovers and mistresses ask that both should know when they cease to love each other, arises much less from a wish to be warned of the cessation of love, than from a desire to be assured that they are beloved although no one denies it. (1665, No. 303.)

LXII.—The most just comparison of love is that of a fever, and we have no power over either, as to its violence or its duration. (1665, No. 305.)

LXIII.—The greatest skill of the least skilful is to know how to submit to the direction of another. (1665, No. 309.)

LXIV.—We always fear to see those whom we love when we have been flirting with others. (1674, No. 372.)

LXV.—We ought to console ourselves for our faults when we have strength enough to own them. (1674, No. 375.)

SECOND SUPPLEMENT.
REFLECTIONS, EXTRACTED FROM MS. LETTERS
IN THE ROYAL LIBRARY.*

*A La Bibliotheque Du Roi, it is difficult at present (June 1871) to assign a name to the magnificent collection of books in Paris, the property of the nation.

LXVI.—Interest is the soul of self-love, in as much as when the body deprived of its soul is without sight, feeling or knowledge, without thought or movement, so self-love, riven so to speak from its interest, neither sees, nor hears, nor smells, nor moves; thus it is that the same man who will run over land and sea for his own interest becomes suddenly paralyzed when engaged for that of others; from this arises that sudden dulness and, as it were, death, with which we afflict those to whom we speak of our own matters; from this also their sudden resurrection when in our narrative we relate something concerning them; from this we find in our conversations and business that a man becomes dull or bright just as his own interest is near to him or distant from him. (*Letter To Madame De Sablé, Ms., Fol.* 211.)

LXVII.—Why we cry out so much against maxims which lay bare the heart of man, is because we fear that our own heart shall be laid bare. (*Maxim* 103, MS., fol. 310.)

LXVIII.—Hope and fear are inseparable. (*To Madame De Sablé, Ms., Fol.* 222, MAX. 168.)

LXIX.—It is a common thing to hazard life to escape dishonour; but, when this is done, the actor takes very little pain to make the enterprise succeed in which he is engaged, and certain it is that they who hazard their lives to take a city or to conquer a province are better officers, have more merit, and wider and more useful, views than they who merely expose themselves to vindicate their honour; it is very common to find people of the latter class, very rare to find those of the former. (*Letter To M. Esprit, Ms., Fol.* 173, MAX. 219.)

LXX.—The taste changes, but the will remains the same. (*To Madame De Sablé, Fol.* 223, *Max.* 252.)

LXXI.—The power which women whom we love have over us is greater than that which we have over ourselves. (*To The Same, Ms., Fol. 211, Max.* 259)

LXXII.—That which makes us believe so easily that others have defects is that we all so easily believe what we wish. (*To The Same, Ms., Fol. 223, Max.* 397.)

LXXIII.—I am perfectly aware that good sense and fine wit are tedious to every age, but tastes are not always the same, and what is good at one time will not seem so at another. This makes me think that few persons know how to be old. (*To The Same, Fol. 202, Max.* 423.)

LXXIV.—God has permitted, to punish man for his original sin, that he should be so fond of his self-love, that he should be tormented by it in all the actions of his life. (*Ms., Fol. 310, Max. 494.*)

LXXV.—And so far it seems to me the philosophy of a lackey can go; I believe that all gaity in that state of life is very doubtful indeed. (*To Madame De Sablé, Fol. 161, Max. 504.*)

[In the maxim cited the author relates how a footman about to be broken on the wheel danced on the scaffold. He seems to think that in his day the life of such servants was so miserable that their merriment was very doubtful.]

THIRD SUPPLEMENT

[The fifty following Maxims are taken from the Sixth Edition of the *Pensées De La Rochefoucauld,* published by Claude Barbin, in 1693, more than twelve years after the death of the author (17th May, 1680). The reader will find some repetitions, but also some very valuable maxims.]

LXXVI.—Many persons wish to be devout; but no one wishes to be humble.

LXXVII.—The labour of the body frees us from the pains of the mind, and thus makes the poor happy.

LXXVIII.—True penitential sorrows (mortifications) are those which are not known, vanity renders the others easy enough.

LXXIX.—Humility is the altar upon which God wishes that we should offer him his sacrifices.

LXXX.—Few things are needed to make a wise man happy; nothing can make a fool content; that is why most men are miserable.

LXXXI.—We trouble ourselves less to become happy, than to make others believe we are so.

LXXXII.—It is more easy to extinguish the first desire than to satisfy those which follow.

LXXXIII.—Wisdom is to the soul what health is to the body.

LXXXIV.—The great ones of the earth can neither command health of body nor repose of mind, and they buy always at too dear a price the good they can acquire.

LXXXV.—Before strongly desiring anything we should examine what happiness he has who possesses it.

LXXXVI.—A true friend is the greatest of all goods, and that of which we think least of acquiring.

LXXXVII.—Lovers do not wish to see the faults of their mistresses until their enchantment is at an end.

LXXXVIII.—Prudence and love are not made for each other; in the ratio that love increases, prudence diminishes.

LXXXIX.—It is sometimes pleasing to a husband to have a jealous wife; he hears her always speaking of the beloved object.

XC.—How much is a woman to be pitied who is at the same time possessed of virtue and love!

XCI.—The wise man finds it better not to enter the encounter than to conquer.

XCII.—It is more necessary to study men than books.

XCIII.—Good and evil ordinarily come to those who have most of one or the other.

XCIV.—The accent and character of one's native country dwells in the mind and heart as on the tongue. (*Repitition Of Maxim* 342.)

XCV.—The greater part of men have qualities which, like those of plants, are discovered by chance. (*Repitition Of Maxim* 344.)

XCVI.—A good woman is a hidden treasure; he who discovers her will do well not to boast about it. (*See Maxim* 368.)

XCVII.—Most women do not weep for the loss of a lover to show that they have been loved so much as to show that they are worth being loved. (*See Maxim* 362.)

XCVIII.—There are many virtuous women who are weary of the part they have played. (*See Maxim* 367.)

XCIX.—If we think we love for love's sake we are much mistaken. (*See Maxim* 374.)

C.—The restraint we lay upon ourselves to be constant, is not much better than an inconstancy. (*See Maxim* 369, 381.)

CI.—There are those who avoid our jealousy, of whom we ought to be jealous. (*See Maxim* 359.)

CII.—Jealousy is always born with love, but does not always die with it. (*See Maxim* 361.)

CIII.—When we love too much it is difficult to discover when we have ceased to be beloved.

CIV.—We know very well that we should not talk about our wives, but we do not remember that it is not so well to speak of ourselves. (*See Maxim* 364.)

CV.—Chance makes us known to others and to ourselves. (*See Maxim* 345.)

CVI.—We find very few people of good sense, except those who are of our own opinion. (*See Maxim* 347.)

CVII.—We commonly praise the good hearts of those who admire us. (*See Maxim* 356.)

CVIII.—Man only blames himself in order that he may be praised.

CIX.—Little minds are wounded by the smallest things. (*See Maxim* 357.)

CX.—There are certain faults which placed in a good light please more than perfection itself. (*See Maxim* 354.)

CXI.—That which makes us so bitter against those who do us a shrewd turn, is because they think themselves more clever than we are. (*See Maxim* 350.)

CXII.—We are always bored by those whom we bore. (*See Maxim* 352.)

CXIII.—The harm that others do us is often less than that we do ourselves. (*See Maxim* 363.)

CXIV.—It is never more difficult to speak well than when we are ashamed of being silent.

CXV.—Those faults are always pardonable that we have the courage to avow.

CXVI.—The greatest fault of penetration is not that it goes to the bottom of a matter—but beyond it. (*See Maxim* 377.)

CXVII.—We give advice, but we cannot give the wisdom to profit by it. (*See Maxim* 378.)

CXVIII.—When our merit declines, our taste declines also. (*See Maxim* 379.)

CXIX.—Fortune discovers our vices and our virtues, as the light makes objects plain to the sight. (*See Maxim* 380.)

CXX.—Our actions are like rhymed verse-ends (*Bouts-Rimés*) which everyone turns as he pleases. (*See Maxim* 382.)

CXXI.—There is nothing more natural, nor more deceptive, than to believe that we are beloved.

CXXII.—We would rather see those to whom we have done a benefit, than those who have done us one.

CXXIII.—It is more difficult to hide the opinions we have than to feign those which we have not.

CXXIV.—Renewed friendships require more care than those that have never been broken.

CXXV.—A man to whom no one is pleasing is much more unhappy than one who pleases nobody.

REFLECTIONS ON VARIOUS SUBJECTS, BY THE DUKE DE LA ROCHEFOUCAULD

I. On Confidence.

Though sincerity and confidence have many points of resemblance, they have yet many points of difference.

Sincerity is an openness of heart, which shows us what we are, a love of truth, a dislike to deception, a wish to compensate our faults and to lessen them by the merit of confessing them.

Confidence leaves us less liberty, its rules are stricter, it requires more prudence and reticence, and we are not always free to give it. It relates not only to ourselves, since our interests are often mixed up with those of others; it requires great delicacy not to expose our friends in exposing ourselves, not to draw upon their goodness to enhance the value of what we give.

Confidence always pleases those who receive it. It is a tribute we pay to their merit, a deposit we commit to their trust, a pledge which gives them a claim upon us, a kind of dependence to which we voluntarily submit. I do not wish from what I have said to depreciate confidence, so necessary to man. It is in society the link between acquaintance and friendship. I only wish to state its limits to make it true and real. I would that it was always sincere, always discreet, and that it had neither weakness nor interest. I know it is hard to place proper limits on being taken into all our friends' confidence, and taking them into all ours.

Most frequently we make confidants from vanity, a love of talking, a wish to win the confidence of others, and make an exchange of secrets.

Some may have a motive for confiding in us, towards whom we have no motive for confiding. With them we discharge the obligation in keeping their secrets and trusting them with small confidences.

Others whose fidelity we know trust nothing to us, but we confide in them by choice and inclination.

We should hide from them nothing that concerns us, we should always show them with equal truth, our virtues and our vices, without exaggerating the one or diminishing the other. We should make it a rule never to have half confidences. They always embarrass those who give them, and dissatisfy those who receive them. They shed an uncertain light on what we want hidden, increase curiosity, entitling the recipients to know more, giving them leave to consider themselves free to talk of what they have guessed. It is far safer and more honest to tell nothing than to be silent when we have begun to tell. There are other rules to be observed in matters confided to us, all are important, to all prudence and trust are essential.

Everyone agrees that a secret should be kept intact, but everyone does not agree as to the nature and importance of secrecy. Too often we consult ourselves as to what we should say, what we should leave unsaid. There are few permanent secrets, and the scruple against revealing them will not last for ever.

With those friends whose truth we know we have the closest intimacy. They have always spoken unreservedly to us, we should always do the same to them. They know our habits and connexions, and see too clearly not to perceive the slightest change. They may have elsewhere learnt what we have promised not to tell. It is not in our power to tell them what has been entrusted to us, though it might tend to their interest to know it. We feel as confident of them as of ourselves, and we are reduced to the hard fate of losing their friendship, which is dear to us, or of being faithless as regards a secret. This is doubtless the hardest test of fidelity, but it should not move an honest man; it is then that he can sacrifice himself to others. His first duty is to rigidly keep his trust in its entirety. He should not only control and guard his and his voice, but even his lighter talk, so that nothing be seen in his conversation or manner that could direct the curiosity of others towards that which he wishes to conceal.

We have often need of strength and prudence wherewith to oppose the exigencies of most of our friends who make a claim on our confidence, and seek to know all about us. We should never allow them to acquire this unexceptionable right. There are accidents and circumstances which do not fall in their cognizance; if they complain, we should endure their complaints and excuse ourselves with gentleness, but if they are still unreasonable, we should sacrifice their friendship to our duty, and choose between two inevitable evils, the one reparable, the other irreparable.

II. On Difference of Character.

Although all the qualities of mind may be united in a great genius, yet there are some which are special and peculiar to him; his views are unlimited; he always acts uniformly and with the same activity; he sees distant objects as if present; he comprehends and grasps the greatest, sees and notices the smallest matters; his thoughts are elevated, broad, just and intelligible. Nothing escapes his observation, and he often finds truth in spite of the obscurity that hides her from others.

A lofty mind always thinks nobly, it easily creates vivid, agreeable, and natural fancies, places them in their best light, clothes them with all appropriate adornments, studies others' tastes, and clears away from its own thoughts all that is useless and disagreeable.

A clever, pliant, winning mind knows how to avoid and overcome difficulties. Bending easily to what it wants, it understands the inclination and temper it is dealing with, and by managing their interests it advances and establishes its own.

A well regulated mind sees all things as they should be seen, appraises them at their proper value, turns them to its own advantage, and adheres firmly to its own opinions as it knows all their force and weight.

A difference exists between a working mind and a business-like mind. We can undertake business without turning it to our own interest. Some are clever only in what does not concern them, and the reverse in all that does. There are others again whose cleverness is limited to their own business, and who know how to turn everything to their own advantage.

It is possible to have a serious turn of mind, and yet to talk pleasantly and cheerfully. This class of mind is suited to all persons in all times of life. Young persons have usually a cheerful and satirical turn, untempered by seriousness, thus often making themselves disagreeable.

No part is easier to play than that of being always pleasant; and the applause we sometimes receive in censuring others is not worth being exposed to the chance of offending them when they are out of temper.

Satire is at once the most agreeable and most dangerous of mental qualities. It always pleases when it is refined, but we always fear those who use it too much, yet satire should be allowed when unmixed with spite, and when the person satirised can join in the satire.

It is unfortunate to have a satirical turn without affecting to be pleased or without loving to jest. It requires much adroitness to continue satirical without falling into one of these extremes.

Raillery is a kind of mirth which takes possession of the imagination, and shows every object in an absurd light; wit combines more or less softness or harshness.

There is a kind of refined and flattering raillery that only hits the faults that persons admit, which understands how to hide the praise it gives under the appearance of blame, and shows the good while feigning a wish to hide it.

An acute mind and a cunning mind are very dissimilar. The first always pleases; it is unfettered, it perceives the most delicate and sees the most imperceptible matters. A cunning spirit never goes straight, it endeavours to secure its object by byeways and short cuts. This conduct is soon found out, it always gives rise to distrust and never reaches greatness.

There is a difference between an ardent and a brilliant mind, a fiery spirit travels further and faster, while a brilliant mind is sparkling, attractive, accurate.

Gentleness of mind is an easy and accommodating manner which always pleases when not insipid.

A mind full of details devotes itself to the management and regulation of the smallest particulars it meets with. This distinction is usually limited to little matters, yet it is not absolutely incompatible with greatness, and when these two qualities are united in the same mind they raise it infinitely above others.

The expression "*Bel Esprit*" is much perverted, for all that one can say of the different kinds of mind meet together in the "*Bel Esprit.*" Yet as the epithet is bestowed on an infinite number of bad poets and tedious authors, it is more often used to ridicule than to praise.

There are yet many other epithets for the mind which mean the same thing, the difference lies in the tone and manner of saying them, but as tones and manner cannot appear in writing I shall not go into distinctions I cannot explain. Custom explains this in saying that a man has wit, has much wit, that he is a great wit; there are tones and manners which make all the difference between phrases which seem all alike on paper, and yet express a different order of mind.

So we say that a man has only one kind of wit, that he has several, that he has every variety of wit.

One can be a fool with much wit, and one need not be a fool even with very little wit.

To have much mind is a doubtful expression. It may mean every class of mind that can be mentioned, it may mean none in particular. It may mean that he talks sensibly while he acts foolishly. We may have a mind, but a narrow one. A mind may be fitted for some things, not for others. We may have a large measure of mind fitted for nothing, and one is often inconvenienced with much mind; still of this kind of mind we may say that it is sometimes pleasing in society.

Though the gifts of the mind are infinite, they can, it seems to me, be thus classified.

There are some so beautiful that everyone can see and feel their beauty.

There are some lovely, it is true, but which are wearisome.

There are some which are lovely, which all the world admire, but without knowing why.

There are some so refined and delicate that few are capable even of remarking all their beauties.

There are others which, though imperfect, yet are produced with such skill, and sustained and managed with such sense and grace, that they even deserve to be admired.

III. On Taste.

Some persons have more wit than taste, others have more taste than wit. There is greater vanity and caprice in taste than in wit.

The word taste has different meanings, which it is easy to mistake. There is a difference between the taste which in certain objects has an attraction for us, and the taste that makes us understand and distinguish the qualities we judge by.

We may like a comedy without having a sufficiently fine and delicate taste to criticise it accurately. Some tastes lead us imperceptibly to objects, from which others carry us away by their force or intensity.

Some persons have bad taste in everything, others have bad taste only in some things, but a correct and good taste in matters within their capacity. Some have peculiar taste, which they know to be bad, but which they still follow. Some have a doubtful taste, and let chance decide, their indecision makes them change, and they are affected with pleasure or weariness on their friends' judgment. Others are always prejudiced, they are the slaves of their tastes, which they adhere to in everything. Some know what is good, and are horrified at what is not; their opinions are clear and true, and they find the reason for their taste in their mind and understanding.

Some have a species of instinct (the source of which they are ignorant of), and decide all questions that come before them by its aid, and always decide rightly.

These follow their taste more than their intelligence, because they do not permit their temper and self-love to prevail over their natural discernment. All they do is in harmony, all is in the same spirit. This harmony makes them decide correctly on matters, and form a correct estimate of their value. But speaking generally there are few who have a taste fixed and independent of that of their friends, they follow example and fashion which generally form the standard of taste.

In all the diversities of taste that we discern, it is very rare and almost impossible to meet with that sort of good taste that knows how to set a price on the particular, and yet understands the right value that should be placed on all. Our knowledge is too limited, and that correct discernment of good qualities which goes to form a correct judgment is too seldom to be met with except in regard to matters that do not concern us.

As regards ourselves our taste has not this all-important discernment. Preoccupation, trouble, all that concern us, present it to us in another aspect. We do not see with the same eyes what does and what does not relate to us. Our taste is guided by the bent of our self-love and temper, which supplies us with new views which we adapt to an infinite number of changes and uncertainties. Our taste is no longer our own, we cease to control it, without our consent it changes, and the same objects appear to us in such divers aspects that ultimately we fail to perceive what we have seen and heard.

IV. On Society.

In speaking of society my plan is not to speak of friendship, for, though they have some connection, they are yet very different. The former has more in it of greatness and humility, and the greatest merit of the latter is to resemble the former.

For the present I shall speak of that particular kind of intercourse that gentlemen should have with each other. It would be idle to show how far society is essential to men: all seek for it, and all find it, but few adopt the method of making it pleasant and lasting.

Everyone seeks to find his pleasure and his advantage at the expense of others. We prefer ourselves always to those with whom we intend to live, and they almost always perceive the preference. It is this which disturbs and destroys society. We should discover a means to hide this love of selection since it is too ingrained in us to be in our power to destroy. We should make our pleasure that of other persons, to humour, never to wound their self-love.

The mind has a great part to do in so great a work, but it is not merely sufficient for us to guide it in the different courses it should hold.

The agreement we meet between minds would not keep society together for long if she was not governed and sustained by good sense, temper, and by the consideration which ought to exist between persons who have to live together.

It sometimes happens that persons opposite in temper and mind become united. They doubtless hold together for different reasons, which cannot last for long. Society may subsist between those who are our inferiors by birth or by personal qualities, but those who have these advantages should not abuse them. They should seldom let it be perceived that they serve to instruct others. They should let their conduct show that they, too, have need to be guided and led by reason, and accommodate themselves as far as possible to the feeling and the interests of the others.

To make society pleasant, it is essential that each should retain his freedom of action. A man should not see himself, or he should see himself without dependence, and at the same time amuse himself. He should have the power of separating himself without that separation bringing any change on the society. He should have the power to pass by one and the other, if he does not wish to expose himself to occasional embarrassments; and he should remember that he is often bored when he believes he has not the power even to bore. He should share in what he believes to be the amusement of persons with whom he wishes to live, but he should not always be liable to the trouble of providing them.

Complaisance is essential in society, but it should have its limits, it becomes a slavery when it is extreme. We should so render a free consent, that in following the opinion of our friends they should believe that they follow ours.

We should readily excuse our friends when their faults are born with them, and they are less than their good qualities. We should often avoid to show what they have said, and what they have left unsaid. We should try to make them perceive their faults, so as to give them the merit of correcting them.

There is a kind of politeness which is necessary in the intercourse among gentlemen, it makes them comprehend badinage, and it keeps them from using and employing certain figures of speech, too rude and unrefined, which are often used thoughtlessly when we hold to our opinion with too much warmth.

The intercourse of gentlemen cannot subsist without a certain kind of confidence; this should be equal on both sides. Each should have an appearance of sincerity and of discretion which never causes the fear of anything imprudent being said.

There should be some variety in wit. Those who have only one kind of wit cannot please for long unless they can take different roads, and not both use the same talents, thus adding to the pleasure of society, and keeping the same harmony that different voices and different instruments should observe in music; and as it is detrimental to the quiet of society, that many persons should have the same interests, it is yet as necessary for it that their interests should not be different.

We should anticipate what can please our friends, find out how to be useful to them so as to exempt them from annoyance, and when we cannot avert evils, seem to participate in them, insensibly obliterate without attempting to destroy them at a blow, and place agreeable objects in their place, or at least such as will interest them. We should talk of subjects that concern them, but only so far as they like, and we should take great care where we draw the line. There is a species of politeness, and we may say a similar species of humanity, which does not enter too quickly into the recesses of the heart. It often takes pains to allow us to see all that our friends know, while they have still the advantage of not knowing to the full when we have penetrated the depth of the heart.

Thus the intercourse between gentlemen at once gives them familiarity and furnishes them with an infinite number of subjects on which to talk freely.

Few persons have sufficient tact and good sense fairly to appreciate many matters that are essential to maintain society. We desire to turn away at a certain point, but we do not want to be mixed up in everything, and we fear to know all kinds of truth.

As we should stand at a certain distance to view objects, so we should also stand at a distance to observe society; each has its proper point of view from which it should be regarded. It is quite right that it should not be looked at too closely, for there is hardly a man who in all matters allows himself to be seen as he really is.

V. On Conversation.

The reason why so few persons are agreeable in conversation is that each thinks more of what he desires to say, than of what the others say, and that we make bad listeners when we want to speak.

Yet it is necessary to listen to those who talk, we should give them the time they want, and let them say even senseless things; never contradict or interrupt them; on the contrary, we should enter into their mind and taste, illustrate their meaning, praise anything they say that deserves praise, and let them see we praise more from our choice than from agreement with them.

To please others we should talk on subjects they like and that interest them, avoid disputes upon indifferent matters, seldom ask questions, and never let them see that we pretend to be better informed than they are.

We should talk in a more or less serious manner, and upon more or less abstruse subjects, according to the temper and understanding of the persons we talk with, and readily give them the advantage of deciding without obliging them to answer when they are not anxious to talk.

After having in this way fulfilled the duties of politeness, we can speak our opinions to our listeners when we find an opportunity without a sign of presumption or opinionatedness. Above all things we should avoid often talking of ourselves and giving ourselves as an example; nothing is more tiresome than a man who quotes himself for everything.

We cannot give too great study to find out the manner and the capacity of those with whom we talk, so as to join in the conversation of those who have more than ourselves without hurting by this preference the wishes or interests of others.

Then we should modestly use all the modes above-mentioned to show our thoughts to them, and make them, if possible, believe that we take our ideas from them.

We should never say anything with an air of authority, nor show any superiority of mind. We should avoid far-fetched expressions, expressions hard or forced, and never let the words be grander than the matter.

It is not wrong to retain our opinions if they are reasonable, but we should yield to reason, wherever she appears and from whatever side she comes, she alone should govern our opinions, we should follow her without opposing the opinions of others, and without seeming to ignore what they say.

It is dangerous to seek to be always the leader of the conversation, and to push a good argument too hard, when we have found one. Civility often hides half its understanding, and when it meets with an opinionated man who defends the bad side, spares him the disgrace of giving way.

We are sure to displease when we speak too long and too often of one subject, and when we try to turn the conversation upon subjects that we think more instructive than others, we should enter indifferently upon every subject that is agreeable to others, stopping where they wish, and avoiding all they do not agree with.

Every kind of conversation, however witty it may be, is not equally fitted for all clever persons; we should select what is to their taste and suitable to their condition, their sex, their talents, and also choose the time to say it.

We should observe the place, the occasion, the temper in which we find the person who listens to us, for if there is much art in speaking to the purpose, there is no less in knowing when to be silent. There is an eloquent silence which serves to approve or to condemn, there is a silence of discretion and of respect. In a word, there is a tone, an air, a manner, which renders everything in conversation agreeable or disagreeable, refined or vulgar.

But it is given to few persons to keep this secret well. Those who lay down rules too often break them, and the safest we are able to give is to listen much, to speak little, and to say nothing that will ever give ground for regret.

VI. Falsehood.

We are false in different ways. There are some men who are false from wishing always to appear what they are not. There are some who have better faith, who are born false, who deceive themselves, and who never see themselves as they really are; to some is given a true understanding and a false taste, others have a false understanding and some correctness in taste; there are some who have not any falsity either in taste or mind. These last are very rare, for to speak generally, there is no one who has not some falseness in some corner of his mind or his taste.

What makes this falseness so universal, is that as our qualities are uncertain and confused, so too, are our tastes; we do not see things exactly as they are, we value them more or less than they are worth, and do not bring them into unison with ourselves in a manner which suits them or suits our condition or qualities.

This mistake gives rise to an infinite number of falsities in the taste and in the mind. Our self-love is flattered by all that presents itself to us under the guise of good.

But as there are many kinds of good which affect our vanity and our temper, so they are often followed from custom or advantage. We follow because the others follow, without considering that the same feeling ought not to be equally embarrassing to all kinds of persons, and that it should attach itself more or less firmly, according as persons agree more or less with those who follow them.

We dread still more to show falseness in taste than in mind. Gentleness should approve without prejudice what deserves to be approved, follow what deserves to be followed, and take offence at nothing. But there should be great distinction and great accuracy. We should distinguish between what is good in the abstract and what is good for ourselves, and always follow in reason the natural inclination which carries us towards matters that please us.

If men only wished to excel by the help of their own talents, and in following their duty, there would be nothing false in their taste or in their conduct. They would show what they were, they would judge matters by their lights, and they would attract by their reason. There would be a discernment in their views, in their sentiments, their taste would be true, it would come to them direct, and not from others, they would follow from choice and not from habit or chance. If we are false in admiring what should not be admired, it is oftener from envy that we affix a value to qualities which are good in themselves, but which do not become us. A magistrate is false when he flatters himself he is brave, and that he will be able to be bold in certain cases. He should be as firm and stedfast in a plot which ought to be stifled without fear of being false, as he would be false and absurd in fighting a duel about it.

A woman may like science, but all sciences are not suitable for her, and the doctrines of certain sciences never become her, and when applied by her are always false.

We should allow reason and good sense to fix the value of things, they should determine our taste and give things the merit they deserve, and the importance it is fitting we should give them. But nearly all men are deceived in the price and in the value, and in these mistakes there is always a kind of falseness.

VII. On Air and Manner.

There is an air which belongs to the figure and talents of each individual; we always lose it when we abandon it to assume another.

We should try to find out what air is natural to us and never abandon it, but make it as perfect as we can. This is the reason that the majority of children please. It is because they are wrapt up in the air and manner nature has given them, and are ignorant of any other. They are changed and corrupted when they quit infancy, they think they should imitate what they see, and they are not altogether able to imitate it. In this imitation there is always something of falsity and uncertainty. They have nothing settled in their manner and opinions. Instead of being in reality what they want to appear, they seek to appear what they are not.

All men want to be different, and to be greater than they are; they seek for an air other than their own, and a mind different from what they possess; they take their style and manner at chance. They make experiments upon themselves without considering that what suits one person will not suit everyone, that there is no universal rule for taste or manners, and that there are no good copies.

Few men, nevertheless, can have unison in many matters without being a copy of each other, if each follow his natural turn of mind. But in general a person will not wholly follow it. He loves to imitate. We often imitate the same person without perceiving it, and we neglect our own good qualities for the good qualities of others, which generally do not suit us.

I do not pretend, from what I say, that each should so wrap himself up in himself as not to be able to follow example, or to add to his own, useful and serviceable habits, which nature has not given him. Arts and sciences may be proper for the greater part of those who are capable for them. Good manners and politeness are proper for all the world. But, yet acquired qualities should always have a certain agreement and a certain union with our own natural qualities, which they imperceptibly extend and increase. We are elevated to a rank and dignity above ourselves. We are often engaged in a new profession for which nature has not adapted us. All these conditions have each an air which belong to them, but which does not always agree with our natural manner. This change of our fortune often changes our air and our manners, and augments the air of dignity, which is always false when it is too marked, and when it is not united and amalgamated with that which nature has given us. We should unite and blend them together, and thus render them such that they can never be separated.

We should not speak of all subjects in one tone and in the same manner. We do not march at the head of a regiment as we walk on a promenade; and we should use the same style in which we should naturally speak of different things in the same way, with the same difference as we should walk, but always naturally, and as is suitable, either at the head of a regiment or on a promenade. There are some who are not content to abandon the air and manner natural to them to assume those of the rank and dignities to which they have arrived. There are some who assume prematurely the air of the dignities and rank to which they aspire. How many lieutenant-generals assume to be marshals of France, how many barristers vainly repeat the style of the Chancellor and how many female citizens give themselves the airs of duchesses.

But what we are most often vexed at is that no one knows how to conform his air and manners with his appearance, nor his style and words with his thoughts and sentiments, that every one forgets himself and how far he is insensibly removed from the truth. Nearly every one falls into this fault in some way. No one has an ear sufficiently fine to mark perfectly this kind of cadence.

Thousands of people with good qualities are displeasing; thousands pleasing with far less abilities, and why? Because the first wish to appear to be what they are not, the second are what they appear.

Some of the advantages or disadvantages that we have received from nature please in proportion as we know the air, the style, the manner, the sentiments that coincide with our condition and our appearance, and displease in the proportion they are removed from that point.

Made in the USA
Monee, IL
07 January 2023

24711363R00075